PU [   ] N

LIFE IN [   ] RKS,

by

Don Carter, Geoff Hart, and Joe Kent
with additional material by Ted Brown

Edited by Nick Wellings.

Cover photograph: one of the 'Golden Arrow' cars, probably PHOENIX, being assembled at Preston Park Works, 1951. Left to right: Johnnie Heward, Ted Reynolds, Idris Edwards, with Wally Verrall in the background.
Opposite: Ted Brown working on the cornice of the K-type standard wooden body cars.

PHOENIX under construction at Preston Park in May 1951.

HOW THIS BOOK CAME ABOUT

Don Carter's, Geoff Hart's and Joe Kent's reminiscences of work in the Pullman Car Company shops at Preston Park were originally recorded on tape on various occasions between April and July 1990. We would meet on Wednesday afternoons in the front room of Geoff Hart's house in Brighton, sit round the table with its rather battered portable tape recorder and the reminiscences would just flow. As the sessions went on, with one memory sparking off another, they became more and more animated, with mimicry of personalities and on one occasion helpless tears of laughter.

The tapes were then transcribed, warts and all, with great pains and patience by Maria Hendricks, and then these transcripts were edited into their present form by Nick Wellings. At this stage Don, Geoff and Joe helped remove any errors and it was fascinating to see their faces as their reminiscences began to unfold in front of them.

Joe Kent took most of the original pictures on a little Voigtlander camera. Those illustrations not by Joe Kent are individually acknowledged. Joe's were rephotographed, developed and hand-printed with great expertise by Michael Sullivan.

Words in square brackets [XXXXX] indicate where Nick Wellings has added material in the hope of making things clearer for the reader.

Names of locomotives and individual cars are given in CAPITALS e.g PHOENIX, LATONA, while names of titled trains are in single inverted commas, eg The 'Brighton Belle', The 'Queen of Scots'.

THE PULLMAN WORKS AND ITS CLOSURE

The Pullman Car Company moved its southern maintenance and restoration work to Brighton in 1928, taking over a former London, Brighton and South Coast Railway carriage shed, built in 1898, at Highcroft Villas, north of Lover's Walk Depot. Although four Pullman Cars were built there, most of the Cars were built elsewhere and the Preston Park works was largely responsible for maintenance and repair. The Company and its workshops, offices and facilities were absorbed by the British Railways Board in 1962 and the Preston Park workshops were closed, with some justifiable bitterness on the part of the work-force, in 1963.

The Company was in a sound financial position. Operating profit for 1960 was £130,765. Available capital stood at £373,468 while current assets were £446,279 with healthy revenue reserves of £293,079. But the British Transport Commission was in the mood for 'rationalisation'. Although rumours abounded, this was largely unknown to men or management. A memo from the Managing Director of 26th October 1962 has it, "The expressed intention of the British Transport Commission is to continue Pullman activities and to expand them where appropriate. Our services and staff have earned a high reputation with the travelling public and British Railways will need to call upon all available Pullman energy and expertise." In the light of future events this can only ring a little hollow. But all seemed to be well. A new canteen was opened at Preston Park by Sir John Elliot, Chairman of the Company in 1962 and the final take over (The British Transport Commission having been the sole ordinary shareholder since 1954) from 1st January 1963 went smoothly with most workers being transferred to British Railways employment. But less than three months later a short announcement was made that the works were to close in early 1964. British Railways presented their case for closure on 10th July 1963. A key passage reads:

> "It would have been most surprising, in the light of the railway workshops
> plan as a whole, if the decision had been to retain Preston Park Works whilst
> closing such places as Lancing, a large part of Swindon, Darlington, and many
> other large relatively efficient works, which were well equipped to perform
> similar work.
>
> Although Preston Park has been used for the maintenance of Pullman cars,
> including some of the newer vehicles of steel and plastic construction, there
> are many Pullman cars in use which have never been repaired at Brighton and
> for which arrangements have been made in the past for them to have been
> repaired elsewhere. The closure of the Preston Park Works, therefore, is but an
> extension, albeit to the ultimate conclusion, of a policy which had been
> adopted by the Pullman Car Company in the past."

The National Union of Vehicle Builders, both at regional and local level (Ted Brown was shop steward at Preston Park) put up an energetic fight, even writing to the then Prime Minister, Harold Wilson, and did gain a grudging admission from British Railways that it was not fully aware of what Preston Park works did, but, sadly, it was of no use. British Railways had made up its mind, as the last sentence of the extract above only too ludicrously reveals. The Preston Park Works of the Pullman Car Company were hurriedly closed in November 1963, with the loss of over 100 jobs and their attendant skills.

Nick Wellings, from material provided by Ted Brown.

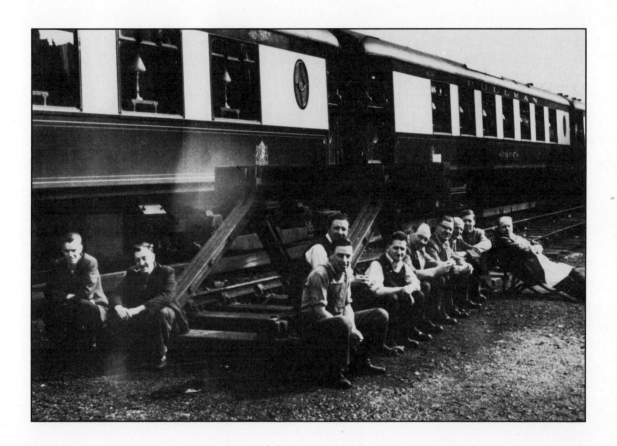

Lunch break in front of Brighton Belle unit 3052: L. to R. Johnie Baldwin, Cyril Miller, Dave Menzies, George Harman, George Yeates, Ron Barnes, Les Green, Ben Farr, Johnnie West, Bert Baldwin. Lunchtime was over when the 1.25 Brighton Belle for Victoria passed the works a few minutes later.

ABOUT THE CONTRIBUTORS

GEOFF HART

I was born in Hertford on June 28th 1919. I served in the Royal Artillery in the Middle East and was one of the Desert Rats. I was demobbed in 1946, married a Brighton girl and have lived in Brighton ever since.

I worked at the Pullman Car Company from 1947 until it closed in 1963. After working at Barclays Bank as a messenger, I retired through ill health in 1973.

Geoff Hart with George, the works cat, who made the works his home.

DON CARTER

I was born and brought up in Brighton. Both my parents came from West Sussex. I was the youngest of a large family of seven boys and three girls. One boy died at the age of six months. Our mother died when I was only six years old. Two of my sisters kept house. My youngest sister, who was knocked down shortly after our mother's death, went to stay with an aunt at Steyning to recuperate and eventually found employment, got married and still lives there.

My Father wanted all us boys to take up a trade. Three of us did so, two became managers in the retail trade and one became a railway guard. As a schoolboy, I was considered average. The kind of boy who's school report always says "could do better if he tried". When I took the eleven plus exam, I did not quite make it to Varndean High, but I was considered good enough for The Brighton Intermediate School which was in York Place at that time. I was there from 1931-1935.

I went straight from school to the Pullman Car Works. It was intended that I should become a Coachbuilders Apprentice. However, a vacancy occurred in the plumbing and pipe fitters department. Eager to leave school, I took it. The man who taught me my trade, Selwyn Smithers, came third in all England when he took his City and Guilds Examination. He kept my nose to the grindstone. In the evenings I went to the Technical College in Richmond Place. The first year I came second in the examinations. Every year after that, I came first, including the years that I went there after the War. I gained a First Class City and Guilds certificate in 1949 and that qualified me to become a member of the 'Worshipful Company of Plumbers' and, if I so wished, to put the letters RP after my name. I also won the JC White prize for the best student and had examples of my sheet copper work put on exhibition.

After the Pullman Works was reduced to a skeleton staff at the outbreak of War, I worked in a local factory and at one time was involved in the making of submarine detection apparatus when the submarine menace was causing heavy losses to our shipping.

In 1943, April 1st of all days, I was called up into the army and served as an infantryman. I served in the Far East in Burma and India. I weighed 9st 6lbs when I joined the army and 7st when I came out of Burma and spent four months in hospital with malaria, dysentery and nervous exhaustion. After a month's leave in England, I was sent to Calcutta. This was the time when Pakistan was being formed. In the course of the quarrel between Muslims and Hindus, murder was carried out wholesale. Five thousand dead bodies on the streets of Calcutta in three days and many more dumped down in the roads. I was present at the Ballygunge sewage station when the 125th body was retrieved.

I was demobbed in 1947. I got married when I was forty five. I knew my wife had a heart problem but I was not expecting to be told seven weeks later that, without open heart surgery she had just two months to live. She lived for six years. I married my present wife eighteen months later. We had known each other since childhood and if I were asked to describe myself I would say that I am a very happy and contented man. I own the roof over my head, I have a nice comfortable bed, a wonderful wife, enough to eat and if my fingers are long enough, I might even find a pound in the dark recesses of my pockets. I am not envious or jealous of anyone, and heaven forbid that I should ever become mean or greedy.

When Dr Beeching made me redundant, I joined the maintenance staff at Sussex University. That would be in April 1963. I was the first one to leave the Pullman Works. I retired in 1979, angina and a trapped nerve in my back causing me to take early retirement.

5th April 1951. Don Carter receives a mock presentation from Stan Bishop, electrician, in front of one of the 'Devon Belle' cars. The 'oscar' was a junk statuette, probably a lamp stand, which somehow found its way into the works.

JOE KENT

Born York Road, Lambeth 8/1918 close to Waterloo Station turntable. Father was skilled carpenter and joiner, mostly in work. Lived in North Camberwell, Old Kent Road, near Bricklayer's Arms goods depot - a large and busy yard and engine shed.

Early education at Raths Road, L.C.C. school (overlooking above yard), then at Bermondsey Central School, L.C.C. (1930-1932). Trade scholarship from there to Shoreditch Technical Institute, Holton until May 1935 learning cabinet making and allied subjects. This qualified as apprenticeship.

Worked in furniture trade workshops in North and East London until called up in Militia in July 1939 for training as gunner at Blandford camp, Dorset. Served in Royal Artillery as Heavy Anti-aircraft gunner in B.E.F. Northern France, October 1939 to June 1940, then static gunsites N.E. England and Clydeside before Egypt, Sicily and Italy 11/41 to 10/45.

London home badly bomb damaged. Mother stayed with her sister and brother-in-law at Patcham. Widowed in 1938 she remarried settling at Patcham to where I came upon demob in January 1946 and still live.

Being shown an 'Argus' advert for staff required at the Preston Pullman Works I applied and was accepted, commencing employment on 20 May 1946 as cabinet maker and general woodworker, having previously re-equipped myself with tools with great difficulty and expense as my old ones were lost in London.

My first job at Preston was helping to finish first class car PLATO ready for the Royal Derby Special, then on JUNO and AURORA and many others including the 'Brighton Belle' and 'Brighton Live Electric' "composite" cars. Much Benchwork came my way also, some of the earliest being the improvisation of office three drawer and kneehole desks from material received from ex NAFFI car counters, blackout shutters etc.

Later more "special" jobs ensued including a mahogany three section board table for the Institute of Transport office in London which we installed and finished on site. With a small mostly regular "gang" (whose charge-hand's widow and daughter now live close to me) I helped carry out many alterations and improvements at the company's Victoria Station offices, Mayfair Office and the Battersea Commissary stores and premises.

I found the Pullman work mainly interesting and enjoyable and had some good workmates some of whom I still keep in touch with.

The work's closure was announced abruptly in March 1963 (though not entirely unexpected). Some of us had the opportunity to transfer to B.R. District Civil Engineers Building Department and after passing the necessary medical exam I began to work on the Brighton

West district at the end of 1963 and soon settled in working at various jobs and locations.

Health beginning to deteriorate I decided to apply for early retirement which came to pass in June 1981 at the age of nearly 63. Just as well perhaps because early in the following year I developed asthma, the treatment of which precipitated cataracts in both eyes and later a damaged retina. The eye troubles are now largely rectified.

At the outset of the asthmatic attack it was suspected that industrial dust and soot may have been responsible for bronchial damage but this could not be proved.

All my working life I was a member of the old Amalgamated Society of Woodworkers, later merged with U.C.A.T.T. having joined in September 1935. I stayed faithful to this although having been urged to move to the National Union of Vehicle Builders while at the Pullman and to the National Union of Railwaymen while at British Rail. I served on works committees for some years.

I never got round to marrying - never seemed to have the time or opportunity! For some years I enjoyed ballroom and Latin dancing once or twice each week (wish I still could!). My old photography hobby still keeps me occupied among other things such as house and garden maintenance, visiting friends, listening to music, etc. Time goes very quickly! I have enjoyed ten years of retirement though not as actively as I could have wished, but I cannot complain. Many of my generation who were born in wartime, raised in the depression years of the thirties and came of age just as the 39-45 conflict began then had to start all over again after it ended, have fared less well!

The Pullman Car Company works at Preston Park in 1962.

CONTENTS

Chapter

THE PULLMAN CAR COMPANY LIMITED.

Telephone:
BRIGHTON 52217/8

Our Ref. ILG/JJ
Your Ref ....

WORKS DEPARTMENT,
HIGHCROFT VILLAS,
PRESTON PARK,
BRIGHTON, 5.

Mr. Thomas G. Carter,
97, Shanklin Road,
Brighton.

2nd July, 1935.

Dear Sir,

Re. your son, Donald Alfred Carter

With reference to your son's recent interview with the above named, we have to advise you that we are prepared to accept your son for training as an apprentice Plumber and Pipe Fitter in our Preston Park Shops.

We understand he was 15 years of age on 15th January 1935 and his apprenticeship will therefore be completed in January 1941.

We will pay weekly, and every week during the period of his apprenticeship, for such time only as he shall work and be employed as an apprentice, wages according to the following scale:-

At 15 years	10/- per week.									
" 16	" 12/-	"	"	plus 1/-	War Bonus or National Award.					
" 17	" 14/6	"	"	" 2/6	"	"	"	"	"	
" 18	" 16/6	"	"	" 4/-	"	"	"	"	"	
" 19	" 19/-	"	"	" 5/6	"	"	"	"	"	
" 20	" 21/6	"	"	" " 7/6	"	"	"	"	"	

The amount paid under the National award is subject to revision from time to time.

At 21 years of age, apprentices if still in our service, are paid full rate less 2d per hour and rise ½d per hour every six months until full rate is reached.

Cont....

-2-

It is understood that during the period of apprenticeship,
you son shall not be, or become a member of any Trade Society
or Trade Union, (except for the purpose of Insurance against
Accident or sickness) or take part in any trade dispute. It is
also understood that he will faithfully serve the full period
of his apprenticeship with us and will only be relased by us under
exceptional circumstances or for medical reasons. We on our part
are free to dispense with his services should his general behaviour
and ability not prove to our satisfaction, or should any circumstance
arise beyond our control.

Everything possible will be done to give the boy a first
class training, and we will endeavour to find him employment on
completion thereof; it must, however, be understood that we are
under no obligation to do so, and retention of his services
thereafter will depend on our labour requirements, his ability
and general conduct during the term of his apprenticeship. In
any case, before providing him with permanent employment we should
wish him to seek at least twelve months experience in some other
works.

Hours of Duty:
    8.0 a.m. to 5.30 p.m. Monday to Friday with one hour for
lunch(12.30 to 1.30 p.m.) and 8.a.m. to 12 noon on Saturday.

We are prepared to start the boy immediately he leaves school
but if you want him to have a holiday befoe commencing, we are
agreeable to this.

Kindly acknowledge and give us your assurance that you accept
the foregoing conditions on behalf of your son, and advise us when
you wish him to commence duty.

                    Yours faithfully,
             for THE PULLMAN CAR COMPANY,

                    J.L.Gilbert,
                    Works Manager.

1. THE BODY SHOP

GENERAL MAINTENANCE

Geoff: We would clock in at seven - thirty in the morning and clock off at six o'clock in the evening.

Joe: I think it was half past five.

Geoff: Yes, half past five later on. But when I first started up there, at Preston Park, it was eight to six. I started up there in 1948. I remember because I was over in the condemned cell at Pentonville [as a warder! - NW]. I came back one day and heard a whisper that I was going to be moved, and I saw the governor and he said, "Well, you're on the short list", and I said "Where to?" and he said it could be Liverpool, Strangeways or Dartmoor. So I said "Where's the likeliest place?". "Dartmoor", he said. I went home and told the wife and she said "Well, if you go to Dartmoor, you go on your own!" So I backed out.

Joe: I started in 1946, May 20th, and we started at eight o'clock then. I know this as there was a train I tried to photograph most mornings as it used to come down about ten minutes to eight. And it was six o'clock we knocked off, right round until about 1962. I know it was six o'clock because I used to hang around some nights, when the light was good, to wait for the 6.12 van train to London Bridge to go up. So instead of going up the steps, I used to hang round the end of the sheds for the 6.12 vans. There was always an interesting engine on it 'Brighton Atlantic', or something like that.

           We didn't build the cars at Preston Park. Various other builders did. Metropolitan Carriage and Wagon Works was the main one. Then there was the Birmingham Carriage Works. And Cravens. But we took over the servicing at Preston Park. And of course any rebuilding. But not all the cars. A lot of the Eastern Region Cars were done at Doncaster. We didn't often see those.

Don: Well, they came down for major stuff.

Joe: Yes, that's right.

Don: After they had messed them up!

Joe:

Exactly. You could always tell theirs because they had gloss painted white ceilings, looked terrible! All the Preston Park cars had matt stippled ceilings, done by two chaps, Alf Clayton and Cyril Pearson, with a stiff brush. And there was a visiting car came in one day, you know those cars had an inch and a quarter, or an inch and a half of camber on them. They weren't dead straight, all those vehicles. You got a camber to allow for the settling of the truss-bars. Well, our chaps used to paint them, and line them out by hand. With a string line from end to end. Now, at Doncaster, some bright spark had used a string line from end to centre, and from centre to end, so of course you had a peak in the lining. And when you were at the end of the car it shouted at you.

Geoff:

And I can remember, when the luggage racks used to come in from Doncaster, they were full of grease, and they were supposed to have been cleaned. Old George Harman used to moan like the dickens over them. Full of grease, they were. God knows how it got on them.

Don:

They say the Romans invented plumbing. I reckon they left their plumbers behind at Doncaster. We never used to worry about their plumbing. We used to strip it out and start all over again.

Joe:

And when you stripped the panelling at the other end of the car, you know it had been to Doncaster because ours used to be marked 'London End', 'Brighton End', 'Main', or 'Spur', and theirs had 'Crimpsall End' or some other fine place.

Geoff:

And do you remember the trouble up at the works when you was taking some pipe down. And you was burning to release the bolts and that. And Jim Bishop had a moan, "That's our job, burning off paint." The trouble it caused! You'd got to burn it to get the bolts free, and the charge-hand painter moaned because you were burning the paint off which was the painters' job.

Joe:

Talking of burning paint off, when they had a proper overhaul, all the wooden cars that is, they had all their paint burned off. Gas flame, it was. And I've got a good snap of a chap called Freddie Gates [see picture over] and he was very good at it. And the panels were up to anything of a couple of feet wide. I've got a picture of him stripping the entire sheet of paint off a car. I just went by when he was doing it, so I said, "Hold it, Fred! Let me get the camera." So I snapped him. And there was Freddie, and the whole sheet of paint rolling off. That was a bit of skilled work, that.

Geoff:

Who was that, Old Fred the Painter? What was his name? He was burning off one day, and of course talking away while he was doing it, and he caught the side of the coach alight.

Fred Gates burning paint off, IN ONE PIECE, from one off the 12 wheel wooden cars, no.96

Joe: Yes, always known as 'Happy' because he never smiled.

Geoff: Got the gas burner, and of course was nattering away, and it caught light. His brother was a foreman. Fred Eliot, yes, Fred Eliot.

Don: Fred was known for his nattering. And when he would be painting on the outside of a vehicle, some of the lads would get inside on the saloons and start an argument, and then they'd pop their heads out and say, "That's right, isn't it, Fred?" and Fred would say "What was that?" So Fred would start, and once he started, you couldn't stop him. So when they had got him going, they would draw back into a further saloon, and for half an hour Fred would talk non-stop! Course he would be varnishing the outside, and the can would be pouring with varnish, the varnish all dripping down the outside.

Joe: And do you remember when they were doing the little gold line. The sort of separating gold line. In the lining. There was Jack Harman started one end, and old Fred Eliot the other. One of them came up above the chalk line and the other had painted along the bottom! A gap in the middle like that, about a quarter of an inch! And of course there was another thing when you were lining out. And working in the car, as you nearly always were, well the car used to move. In the end, they had to get a prop, a car stand or something. You used to get wobbly lines otherwise!

Don: And they had trouble with a vehicle once, a wooden vehicle. They had their piece of string and a nail at each end, stuck on the vestibule ends. And as the string travelled along, they said the centre of the vehicle moved two inches. Course, those vehicles were all built on a camber and it was the camber taking itself up.

Joe: But it was so funny. I was watching them. And of course standing back, you could see what was going to happen. There was Jack Harman coming along on the top of the chalk line and Fred Eliot on the bottom. Course they had a row then. And a couple of very serious looking chaps they were, weren't they? And of course, the other thing, working on those early cars in particular, when you was stripping out, especially those ceiling jobs, you put your coat on, and a choker, and your cap! Those Eastern Region cars were full of soot! There were nine tunnels out of King's Cross. So the cars were full of pungent soot. I think some of it is still down in my lungs now. Just like fine black pepper it was.

Geoff: Yes, that dust!

15

Fred Eliot and Jack Harman at work, painting one of the Brighton BelleThird class cars, 8th May 1951.

Joe: When you had to drop a whole ceiling, you just let it go, got out of the way quick, and waited for the dust to settle. It would never be allowed today. You'd be wearing smog masks and have extractor fans.

Don: When they built those three 'Golden Arrow' cars, they had steel panelling up the roof and all up the sides and some chaps came down from a firm in London and they sprayed it with asbestos, you know to stop the metal drumming in traffic. They never wore masks or anything. So one half of the shop would be like blue smoke, so everybody used to clear up the end and find themselves a job on the bench. But they were spraying this stuff, and the air, well I don't know what it was like down there, but right across the bottom of the shop, it was absolutely clouded. Some chap must have died a horrible death, I should think.

Joe: Well, this is gone thirty years now.

THE BRASS SHOP

Geoff: When the brass fittings were taken off the cars, when the cars came in for repairing and recleaning, all the brass work was brought along to the brass shop. It was then put in tanks of caustic soda and boiled for two or three days. Then it was taken out and put in cold water with half a bottle of acid in. Then it was dipped, put on the brushes and cleaned. It was then dried and it went out after that to the other department for polishing. What I used to do was the dipping. After that it went on to the machines and was polished, buffed and lacquered. That all took place in the brass shop, down the far end, the north end, where the boiler house was.

Joe: Don't forget, when the cars came in, it was the woodmen who took the fittings off.

Geoff: And we had all the screws as well. The brass ones, they were done like the other brass, all in the brass shop. But the oxidised ones had to be re-oxidised.

Joe: When we stripped the cars, they were all put into boxes, all mixed up, en masse.

Top: *The Body Shop Gang outside the works. L. to R.: Stan Cobbett, Ernie Sweetman, Ernie Tamkin, Joe Lowden, Bert Hill, Johnnie Bolch, Bob Crone, Derek Young, Wally Terry and Ted Brown.*

Bottom: *The Trimmers Shop with the Trimming Staff.*

Geoff:	And we did the satin-silver ones too, from the electric cars. But they weren't put in the caustic. We cleaned them up by hand. But the caustic had to be changed, every six months or so. And they were big tanks. Seven feet by two, all lead lined. And for protective wear, you'd have rubber aprons, and rubber gloves. But you never used to use them. Only when you was on the acid. And once or twice I had acid splash in my eyes, so straight away cold water, but never anything serious. And we used to put a pail full of caustic soda crystals in every Monday morning. Then about once a month, we used to have to clean the tank out, and it would be like thick sand at the bottom! That was my job! I didn't have to be told, you just knew when it had to be done. And if a new lad came out with me, I'd tell him how to go on. He'd be attached to me. But, I mean, if it came to it that the tank was due to be changed on a Monday morning, and we got in on a Monday and got talking together and that, then it wasn't done to the following Monday! But, getting back to the brass shop, all the brass, when it had been lacquered, each job was put on the racks. So the whole of the brasswork for one car would be on a particular rack. When the woodmen came to do the cars up, they used to come and get the particular brasswork and take it out, well, the small bits. The large bits somebody in the brass shop would push it out for them on a trolley.
Joe:	Incidentally, when it came off a car, I think Butler used to check it.
Don:	Yes, Jack Butler. He was sort of deputy foreman, wasn't he?
Geoff:	He was deputy to Bristow [Works Foreman].
Don:	He actually used to order timber as well, because he was an expert on timber, and glass, timber and glass. Yes, he was a sort of Deputy Foreman.

THE GANTRY

Joe:	It was a sort of giant cradle, just inside Number 6 road. It went round the sides, and one end of the car, with one end kept open, to let the car be shunted in. Then there was a pulley at the open end, to let that end down. It was used for all sorts of jobs, roofwork, woodwork, general maintenance on the steel cars, cornice work, brackets, any recanvassing that needed doing. All that sort of thing. And of course for the destination board and title board brackets. Ted Durden and Ron Farley were mainly responsible for any roof recanvassing.

Top: The Bodywork Gang. L. to R.: Bill Waddington, Jerry Tanner, Ted Brown, Ted Browning, Bert Hill, unidentified worker in shadow, and Henry Smith.

Bottom: Painters: Back row L.to R.: Alf Reeves, George Izzard, Dennis Watts. Front L.to R.:Jerry Darby, Johnnie Casburn, Cyril Pearson and an unidentified member of the gang. To the left are newly varnished doors waiting to be fitted.

FINISHING THE CARS

Geoff: While we were there, the livery was always chocolate and cream. We never touched any of the 'green' cars, and the electric blue only came in later [1968 -NW]

Joe: And that wretched squashed cauliflower crest!

Geoff: But there was no doubt about it, when those cars were finished up the Pullman [Preston Park Works], they looked MARVELLOUS!

Don: The outside used to shine like glass!

Geoff: All done with straight varnish on the coaches, no elbow grease.

Don: There were eleven coats of paint on first, and the finish up was two coats of coating varnish and then one coat of finishing varnish. And in between coats, they were rubbed down, weren't they?

Geoff: They really looked marvellous. You could stand back and be really proud of it.

Don: You could see your face in it.

Joe: It was a job that was done right. There used to be a chart in the shop. A long panel. From top to bottom, it gave you all the different stages: the lead colour, the filler, the undercoat, half-and-half, the finishing colour.

Don: I think it used to start off: two coats of filler, then two coats of lead colour, then they put the dye on and rubbed it all down.

Joe: Yes, a sort of stain over the top...

Don: Then it had two coats of undercoat, of various colours, two coats of that, and then it had a coat of gloss...

Joe: They put half-and-half on first. They used to call it half-and-half. It was a diluted colour.

Don: Used to use half-and-half in the kitchen sometimes. Half gloss and half matt. But on the outside I think it had two coats of undercoat and one coat of gloss and then three coats of varnish, two coat varnish, one finishing varnish, rubbing down between each.

Geoff: And I have seen some of the fellas there. Their fingers have been raw where they'd been continually rubbing down, you know, what with the water and that.

Joe: And all this was done in the general workshop where all kinds of trades would be going on at the same time. Including the polishers, they had the same trouble. But Mr Gilbert [The Works Manager], he was very strict, not allowing any shunting engine to come into the shop when they were finishing off, because of the smoke. It did on occasions, but not very far, and not very often!

Geoff: Ernie King was one of the French polishers, wasn't he? He was a little short man, his head only just came up to the top of the bench! Someone said they'd put 35 coats of polish on, and he looked at it and said "You've only got 34 on there!" How he ever knew, I don't know. And this chap admitted he'd done it with only 34 coats! He was a little man, so you wouldn't think he would have noticed it. But to notice there was one coat missing.

Joe: And bench work still had to be done when the finishing was going on. There were a couple of benches at the top end of the shop, some over the far side, back of number one road, and the main bench was down at the office end.

Don: And the drying process for this was one coat a day, so it was dry the following day. Usually the cars went right through, continuously, so it could take twelve to fourteen days, from start to finish. We used to watch the painters as they were progressing and thought, "Oh well, we'd better get up there and do our bit now" [plumbing, fittings, etc - NW]. As soon as the paint was on, we were ready to go, that sort of thing.

Joe: The usual panic was getting the insides fitted out, really. You used to get, and we all know this, you used to get fellas working on top of each other then. You'd get the polishers trying to finish off, we'd be trying to finish fixing the seats and the brassware. Don and company would be in the kitchen, and painters were in there trying to paint the kitchen at the same time. And the gas men in there as well, trying to get the stoves finished.

Don: When you think about how many men you can get in a phone box... Well, how many men can you get in a toilet? Because I'd be laying under a wash basin, there'd be a French polisher standing over me, polishing away. The electrician would be in there, putting the lights in...

Joe: And me in the corner, waiting to get in, carrying a table...

Don:	And you didn't dare leave to go to the toilet, because if you did, your place'd be taken.
Geoff:	But it used to get done.
Joe:	Yes, it used to be done.
Don:	But the funny thing is that no one lost his temper.
Geoff:	I can't remember it ever happening.
Don:	You'd be pulling somebody's leg all the time.
Joe:	Just lots of good-natured banter!

Rubbing down one of the standard K-type cars.

Alf Payne, Metal Polisher, in front of one of the ambulance cars, after receiving his retirement present. Alfie was well-known for his ability never to smile, not even on retirement!

2. PERSONALITIES

CHARLIE BRISTOW

Geoff: Charlie Bristow, he was the works foreman.

Don: He was a little short man, like a garden gnome. We used to call him 'The gnome with the dome'! But he didn't suffer from 'little man's disease'.

Geoff: He was a Mason. He used to come down the Pullman with his bag! He was one of those... what d'you call them?... grandmasters or something. But, unfortunately, he got knocked down getting on a bus. It wasn't at work. It was the driver of this car. Charlie, he was going to get on the bus and this car hit him. And do you remember when a couple of American boats were down here. There was a report about it in the *Evening Argus* about two girls swimming out to them. One of them was Bristow's daughter. 1962 or 1963 it was.

Joe: Or the beginning of '64.

Don: He came from Lancing as a tradesman, and then he went back to Lancing. But there was trouble between him and Jack Butler. I think the real history of it was that Jack Butler was foreman during the War and there was only a skeleton staff there during the War. There was a planer in the wood machine shop and something went wrong with it. Jack Butler tried to repair it. And then they started it up, there was a loud bang, and bits of it went flying through the floor. And Jack Butler was a religious man, see, and Old Sedcole [Chief Engineer, London], being a Geordie, used to lay his tongue to a bit. Jack Butler says to him, "I don't swear, Mr Sedcole. So I don't see why you should swear at me." And from that day on, Jack Butler got nowhere. So there was a bit of resentment there, see, and I think some rubbed off on Charlie Bristow.

Joe: I last saw Charlie Bristow at Brighton Station. That was 26th June 1971, the day of the final closure of the Kemp Town Branch. He was in poor health then. Result of his accident, I believe. And I think he finally worked at East Croydon Booking Office, or was attached to it in some way. Supposed to be known as BR's richest booking clerk as he kept his foreman's grade and pay! But he was a capable foreman. No major hiccups as I recall. Minor things, of course, disagreements here and there, but nothing that couldn't be sorted out.

DICK CANNON

Don: Before the war there was a chap in the Brass Shop, fella called Dick Cannon. He
            was a shipbuilder, and brass finishing is a trade in shipbuilding. When he came
            to work up the Pullman, everyone was amazed at his qualifications. He had so
            many of them and he was an absolute genius really, but he was a peculiar chap.
            Now, obviously, up North, if you had a job then, you hung onto it and made sure
            no one took it off you. And if you went to speak to him, and he was doing
            something on the vice, and you leaned over him, then he hunched up and
            wouldn't let you see what he was doing! And you know the lock-spindle on the
            ordinary car door handle, well, old Dick Cannon could file a piece of that without
            putting any square angle on it, and he would file a piece of that lock-spindle, 18"
            high, and it would stand up. It wouldn't rock at all! An absolute craftsman that
            bloke, but he was a bit... peculiar. And he usually talked in a big deep voice, but
            the only one who would have anything to do with him was old Sel Smithers, and
            that was because Sel Smithers had come third in an All-England competition,
            and he recognised Dick Cannon as a real tradesman. And Dick would come in
            and say, "The trouble today is people don't want to work. All they think about
            is the football pools". Then one day he came in and said, "The problem is my
            wife is trying to poison me!"

ALF PAYNE

Geoff: There was an old chap who used to work in the Brass Shop, and if he walked
            to work, he used to walk from London Street to Highcroft Villas. If he got
            to the top of the steps and it was 7.25, then he knew he couldn't get down
            the steps into the works to clock in by 7.30, so he would turn round and go
            home, and he wouldn't work that day, just because he'd been late.

JACK HARMAN

Joe: Jack Harman didn't turn up one day and so I said to him "What happened to
            you yesterday?" and he said,"Well I got on my bike, and do you know, it took
            me the wrong way, it took me up the allotment!"

Don: He had a favourite habit of disappearing some Monday afternoons. He went on the pier
            fishing. I think his wife had money. I tell you, he wasn't hard up for a penny, Old Jack.

ALF GEE AND TED BROWNING

Joe: Yes, there was a lot of rivalry between these two. They were chargehands, when we were doing the 'Devon Belle' Observation Car.

Don: That's right... Alf Gee was known as 'Dad' and Ted Browning he was called 'Jockey'.

Joe: I don't know how that came about. Alf's name for Ted was 'Klegs'.

Don: As though he'd been riding a horse and forgotten to get off it. But he had several names. He had a fairly big head, bald, and his scalp used to go very dark in the sun, so somebody nick-named him 'mahogany-bonce' !

Joe: Never see him without his cap!

Don: And he was called 'Seretse Khama'. He had about four or five nick-names.

Joe: There was a photograph in an exhibition at the Pavilion four or five years ago, and I had to laugh when I saw it. He was included in it. And the only time I have ever seen him without his cap on was in this photo. I said then it's a good job he's not alive to see this!

Geoff: I think I've never seen a man deteriorate as Alf Gee deteriorated. He had retired of course, but I was in Sainsbury's one day and he came in. He'd had a stroke and it was difficult for him to take two or three steps. He was a big man too, but he'd gone to nothing.

Don: Of course, I think a lot of his trouble was that he used to go working of a night. Laurie Wilkinson used to help him.

LAURIE WILKINSON

Joe: Laurie Wilkinson was known as the moonlight builder, wasn't he, he built his own house up The Droveway.

Don: Funnily enough, he had a letter come through his door one day, addressed to 'The Moonlight Builder'. And one night the police picked him up in Dyke Road, about 11.30, as he was putting a new sash-cord in. Half past eleven at night! Then one time he was helping Alf Gee put a big extension on the back of his house, and it got to about midnight and old Alf said to him, "Don't you think it's about time we packed up?" But Laurie said to him. "Well, if you want to, but I'll go home and probably have a couple of hours in my garage."

Joe: And there was that time he was going up to the Coronation, and he made a couple of things to stand on, and he took them up, so he could see above the crowd. Knocked them up from paint cans and string!

Don: He was a good tradesman, tho'.

Joe: He was indeed. He really worked out those upstairs offices up the Pullman.

Don: Then he had to make a big skylight once, up at Gilbert's house, terrific great thing it was. He told me he was going to fit it at the weekend. He'd built his own house by then, so he seemed quite capable, you know. Anyway, he went out there and got up on this roof to do the job. Apparently Gilbert wanted this room for his children to play table tennis in, but unfortunately, the king posts that held the roof up were in the way. So he sawed them off. God knows what happened to the roof!

GEORGE RILEY

Geoff: And do you remember George Riley, used to be on the polishers? I was talking to him one day and I told him I'd been reading a bit in the paper about the Dambusters. He said, "What about the Dambusters?". So I told him to read it. And he said "I was there". He was one of the Dambusters! "Well, that's all wrong," he said, "because the squadron leader of that particular plane, didn't bring the plane back, it crashed into the sea." Then he said, "I was on that plane." He wrote to the paper and complained, and he got some money for it, they sent him a cheque.

Don: He had the Distinguished Flying Medal, you know.

Joe: I knew he'd been in the RAF. He took over the sweet shop in the works, just a case on one of the benches. Like an old school tuck shop, selling sweets, crisps, stuff like that. And Ernie Sweetman worked on that as well!

Don: And he belonged to the RAF Volunteer reserve.

Geoff: Last I heard he was at Gatwick, in the control tower.

L. to R.: Les Nichols, Ted Browning, Ernie Wenham, Wally Verrall, Jack Tate and Bert Hill, at work on one of the 'Golden Arrow' cars, no 3280, 16th May 1951,.

ALF WATERER

Joe:
Alf worked in the stores. He was a marvel too, old Alf. He was in charge of the stores and it didn't matter, whatever you wanted, you asked him, and he'd know just where to go. He was one of the characters.

Don:
He came down from London with a firm, but he lodged here. He lived with his two sisters, in Lavender Hill. He used to go home at weekends and one night in the week, Wednesdays I think, and he'd come back early Thursday morning. He had the most fantastic memory of any man I have ever known. You could go to the stores with a requisition, and he would write the stock number on! So one day I asked him. "Do you ever have to go and look up a stock number?" He said, "Well I might have to go and look once in six months." And probably some of the stuff he brought out hadn't been asked for for a year! It might be any old item but Alf would know. And he was as strong as a horse, that bloke. One day old Jesse Chitty went down the stores and was giving a lot of old buck to him, so he leaned over and grabbed Jesse and dragged him bodily straight over the counter. And Jesse wasn't a small fella, either.

Geoff:
You know those old rolls of copper, no, lead. I have seen Alf pick up a roll and I reckon it weighed four hundred weight. Pick it up just like that. It usually took three or four people to lift a roll. Marvellous old man, he was.

Don:
And so inoffensive, very quiet, and very well mannered.

Geoff:
And one day he said to me, "Here, take this. You might get a pound or two for it." It was half a groat! I took it down to the museum and they told me it was damaged and all out of shape and not worth anything. Well, I was at Barclays at that time and a man used to come in, name of Taylor from Hove, a collector. I said I'd got half a groat and he said, "I'll give you £5 for it" and he did. He gave me £5. Now I often think if he could give me £5 for it without looking at it, what it was really worth.

Don:
Alf came in one day and said to me, "This is interesting." And he showed me a paper he had found, dated 1905, about Falmer Waterworks, you know, back of Saunders Park, bottom of Hollingdean Road. They wanted to shut it down because people said a lot of water was flowing in there from the cemetery and they were frightened it was contaminated. So the authorities wouldn't allow a new one built until the old one was shut down. Since the War they've opened it up again, but they're not using the old beam engine. But he was a very interesting man, Old Alf.

Joe: I used to like to talk to him because he showed a bit of interest in the old cars. He opened up, then. He was one of the ones who could remember the old sleeping car BALMORAL (assembled Derby 1883, now awaiting restoration - NW). He had such a memory.

THE DETECTIVE

Geoff: Who was the detective who worked in the office on No.1 Platform, Brighton Station, retired detective? Stacey, wasn't it? He lived in Bear Road. He was an old Brighton detective, and he was one of these men who'd only got to look at you, and you got time! He was one of the old original ones. You have heard of the copper on the white horse during the General Strike [1926 - NW], Inspector Chick, who killed a man with his truncheon. Stacey was with him too during that strike.

Don: I remember Stacey because he had an allotment next to us.

Geoff: He used to sit in that office, and he'd got "Detective" written all over him. You only had to look at him and you'd know. He had a son who went to Nottingham. And Stacey went up there about three years ago, had a heart attack and died.

SHOW-BIZ

Joe: There was a lot of work in 1948. We were all kept very busy as they were trying to get the trains back on after the war.

Don: And they wanted the 'Queen of Scots' back on, that was what they were after.

Joe: Not that it was the first back after the War. That was the 'Brighton Belle'. Then the 'Golden Arrow', I think.

Don: Where did it go back on?

Geoff: I can tell you when it was... when did "Nicholas Silver" win the Grand National? Wally Terry, he was taking bets when the race was half way running, and people were betting on "Nicholas Silver." That was when what's-his-name chased Wally Terry into the toilets!

31

Joe: Or was it "Sheila's Cottage?"

Geoff: No, not "Sheila's Cottage." That won when I was on my honeymoon [1946 - NW]. I know because there was a standing joke about it!

Don: When the 'Queen of Scots' was eventually got back on the rails (1948 - NW), the company allowed so many of us to travel on it, not doing any work or anything, but just to travel on it. And there was big propaganda about it. They had three young Rank starlets on it. Rona Anderson, and I think Gordon Jackson was with her.

Geoff: Yes, Rona Anderson was on it. She married Gordon Jackson. And a regular traveller on the 'Brighton Belle' was Anna Neagle. She was married to Herbert Wilcox. But she died a little while ago, two or three years ago. And everybody, to a man, used to disappear when the 'Belle' came in, if Max Miller was on it. They wouldn't go near him.

Don: But Jean Kent was the one who had to wave the green flag to get the 'Queen of Scots' away. And it was supposed to pull up the platform just a little way, and wait for her to get on it. But it just went off and left her on the platform!

Geoff: And of course there was Lawrence Olivier, a regular on the 'Belle.'

Joe: And the actress who lives in Brighton now, has done for years, Dora Bryan.

Geoff: And do you know that chap who used to live in Viaduct Road, I can remember someone shouting out to him one day, "What's the time?" And he said, "If you've got the time, I've got the money." It was Larry Adler, riding a bike up there!

4th July,1963.

Dear Mr. Brown,

Thank you for your letter of the 2nd July which I found very interesting - the more so as you were present at the Westminster rally last week.

I will pass your comments to the department at Transport House which deals with policy so that it can be taken into account in relation to any future propaganda.

Yours sincerely,

Harold Wilson

Mr. E. J. Brown,
The Pullman Car Company,
 Shop Secretary, N.U.V.B.,
Highcroft Villas, Brighton 5.

STRIKERS PLAN BIG BANNER MARCH

Vehicle Men Claim 3d.

BRIGHTON'S strikers, members of the National Union of Vehicle Builders, will stage a protest march and mass demonstration next Wednesday.

They plan to march through the town with banners to an open-air meeting on the Level.

This decision was taken at a well-attended meeting on the Level, when the Strike Committee reported "no change" in the situation. It was announced that nearly 450 men are on strike.

A resolution pledging support to the Executive Council in calling the strike was carried with no dissentients.

The strike committee announced that they had started a strike fund to relieve members suffering financial hardship.

The strike is now in its third week. The men are claiming a pay increase of 3d. an hour.

Only three of the 450 members of the local branch of the Union have refused to strike.

Brighton, Hove and District Trades Council yesterday evening unanimously decided to endorse a resolution of their Executive Committee recommending all affiliated trade unions to assist the strikers financially. They set an example by donating £5 to the strikers' relief funds. A spontaneous collection among the Council delegates realised more than £3.

---

300 STRIKERS STILL OUT

Men Object to New Agreements

DESPITE the breakdown of local negotiations, the representatives of the 300 members of the National Union of Vehicle Builders who are still on strike hope that work will be resumed on Monday.

The men struck on Monday, April 5, on the orders of their union, who demanded a 3d. an hour wage increase. As neither the Ministry of Labour nor the employers would consider negotiations while the strike was on, the union's executive committee ordered the members back to work on Wednesday.

Some local men went back but 300 employees of Messrs. Thomas Harrington, of Old Shoreham-road, Hove, remained out. According to Mr S. Hearne, the shop steward, Harrington's workers found that the firm were imposing new conditions and required each man to sign an agreement. Following a meeting at the works gates, it was decided to refuse to return.

"We could not accept any fresh agreements," said Mr Hearne. "We called in union officials to have talks with Harrington's, but the firm were adamant, although we presented ourselves for work on Thursday morning.

"Now the dispute has been referred to higher authority, and we hope for a settlement over the week-end. Our attitude has been perfectly reasonable, and we are sorry that 2,500 man-hours a day are being lost through no fault of our own."

Messrs. Harrington's declined to comment on the dispute.

Work at the Pullman Car Company, the only other local firm affected by the national strike, resumed on Wednesday.

VEHICLE BUILDERS' STRIKE CONTINUES

A well-attended meeting of the local members of the National Union of Vehicle Builders, who are on strike for a 3d. an hour increase in pay, was addressed by London officials of the union at the Labour Club, London-road, on Thursday. This was the second mass meeting in Brighton since the strike began on Monday, April 5, and again 100 per cent. support was guaranteed to the executive committee of the union.

Employees of Messrs. Nicholls, transport contractors, of North-road, held a social evening and concert at the Richmond Hotel on Saturday evening. The effort was to raise funds to assist the relatives of the late Mr W. Rich, a former colleague, who died as the result of an accident, and Mr Johnson, who has retired through ill-health. The concert was organised by Mr Dan Hall, and the programme was given by the Hit and Jep variety company with Mr H. E. Hitchin as M.C. The artistes were thanked by Mr Scott, chairman of the firm's social committee.

BRIGHTON STRIKE IS OVER

STRIKE of 220 workers employed by Thos. Harrington, Ltd., Hove, is over. They will return to work on Monday.

Following a meeting of trade union officials and representatives of the firm and a subsequent mass meeting of the men the union say a satisfactory agreement has been reached.

Mr. S. J. Hearne, shop steward, told the Evening Argus that conditions laid down by the firm had been dispensed with.

When the country-wide strike of the National Union of Vehicle Workers for 3d. an hour increase was called off by the National Executive, the Hove men refused last Wednesday to return to work. They alleged that Thos. Harrington, Ltd., endeavoured to impose certain conditions on the men.

Mr. Clifford Harrington, a director of the firm, told the Evening Argus to-day, "We are offering employment to people we are able to employ."

STRIKERS PLAN MARCH

THE 450 Brighton members of the National Union of Vehicle Builders, who on Monday began the fourth week of their strike for a 3d. an hour increase in pay, common with 22,000 fellow unionists throughout the country, are to organise a mass demonstration march next Wednesday afternoon.

Carrying home-made banners, they will march from the Level to the north end of the Royal Pavilion and back, and a mass meeting will follow.

Using a delivery cart, shafts rampant, as a platform, officials of the Brighton strike committee addressed a mass meeting of strikers on the Level on Wednesday, and told them that the offer of financial help from other trade unions in the district had been accepted. The men are being paid £2 a week by their union.

An effect of the strike earlier in the week was the "temporary suspension" of about 50 panel-beaters, who are members of the National Union of Sheet Metal Workers, by Messrs. Thomas Harrington's, whose 300 coach-builders have been "out" since April 5.

Owing to lack of work, it was proposed by Messrs. Harrington's to suspend some of their panel-beaters, but, according to Mr B. G. Perry, joint secretary of the vehicle builders' strike committee, by pre-arrangement all the men asked for their "cards."

3. THE STRIKE OF 1948

Geoff: The Management offered us sixpence an hour extra and Harding (F.D.M. Harding, OBE, Managing Director) said, "Well, if you only get three pence, you've gained threepence by it." But oh no, they wouldn't have that. No, they went on strike, George Perry was there, and his brother, Bill. At any rate, we went out on strike. Out for three weeks, then suddenly we went back to work, no explanation or anything. And we got a penny an hour extra!

Joe: It was a mistake from start to finish.

Geoff: And we worked Saturdays and Sundays after that, to make up. We lost an awful lot of money.

Joe: And after that the notices went out. Blokes were getting the sack. But I think they took some more chaps on about that time, didn't they.

Geoff: Yes, oh yes.

Don: Incidentally, before the war, it was non-union. But when I got back, and I didn't get back until 1947, they'd made it a closed shop, but they hadn't included our department, the plumbers, and although I was allowed to go to the committee meetings, that was it as far as I was concerned. So anyway, when the strike came about, every time I used to raise anything, they used to say, "You're not party to the agreement." So when this strike came, Perry came up to me... It was Perry, wasn't it?

Geoff: Yes, George Perry.

Don: Well Perry came up to me and said, "I suppose all of you lot are coming out with us." Well, I'd seen my union representative the night before, so I told Perry, "No, I wasn't coming out. I wasn't 'party to the agreement'."

Joe: I was more or less an odd man out as well, because I was in the Amalgamated Society of Woodworkers, as it was then. I never changed over, stuck with it, stayed loyal. One or two didn't like me over there, Perry didn't in fact. But when the strike was on, I went to see my local secretary and asked him what I should do and he said, "You'd better come out, and we'll pay you." So that was three weeks holiday. But nobody liked Perry. He was very unpopular.

Geoff: I saw he died a few months ago. I knew it was him by the address that was given. I remember coming home one night from the pictures with my wife, one Saturday night, and she got right up the end of the trolley bus and we used to get out at the Stanford Arms. George Perry's brother, Bill Perry, was with his wife and some others who'd just come out of the pub, and he said to my wife, "Come on you, move your bloody self!" So I got hold of him, spun him round and said, "That's my wife your talking to!" He shut up after that! Then he would come up the works with some bits and pieces, and he's say, "Would you clean these up for me?" And one day he came up with some tiny little bits, you could hardly hold them, and he brought them back and said, "That's not good enough. There's a scratch on it!" So I said, "You bloody well clean them yourself, then!"

Don: After I'd told George Perry that I wasn't "party to the agreement", so I couldn't be "party to the strike", I had a word with my chap and he said, "You'll stop work when I tell you to." But anyway in the end we were locked out, so that saved all the arguments.

Geoff: It was a lot of nonsense.

Joe: A strike over nothing as far as we were concerned.

Geoff: It was a surprise when it happened, though. There was no mention of it. Then they suddenly came round with some papers saying you could vote for a strike if you wished. Of course, all the chaps at the brass shop were putting a cross at "NO". It went through. The party came down at 12.15 and by 1.00 we were on strike.

Don: The origin of the strike was the Union of Coach Builders' people who worked at Harringtons [the ex-coach builders]. They worked under what they called the "model agreement". It was a separate agreement altogether, but because the Union of Coach Builders at Harrington's said, "Pull the Pullman people out", out we came, because a lot of our chaps in the body shop had been through Harrington's. And they had a bit of a hot-head as shop steward.

[The "agreement" was "The United Kingdom Joint Wages Agreement" of the National Union of Vehicle Builders - NW].

4. SHENANIGANS

Geoff: One day, it was on a Friday, as on the Saturday I was going to Looe on holiday, old Gilbert said to me, "Hart, I've got a chair round the French Polishers being done. Will you take it up and put it in my car?" So I carried it up and put it in his car. I came back down. There was Bert Wickham and myself and we were suddenly surrounded by blokes. "What's this?" I said. "We're railway police," they said. "You've just carried a chair up there." "Yes," I said, "Mr. Gilbert's" "And who's Mr. Gilbert?" "The Works Manager." And they took us up the top and said. "Right now, you sit in there." And they sat us in this police car, and they took Bert's statement. Then they said, "Right, we'll have yours now." "No you won't," I said, "I've got nothing to state, seeing what I was doing I was doing on orders." Then the Chief of Police, Dieppe was his name, came down and asked what the trouble was. And they said, "This chap refuses to make a statement." "Well that's his business, isn't it?" he said. "All right, take them back down the works again." So they took us down and put us in the old canteen. "Now, where's Mr. Gilbert?" he said. "I'll go and find him." "No you won't," they said, "You sit there!" Then Gilbert comes round with Charlie Bristow, "What's this trouble?" he said. "This man's been caught taking a chair." "Yes, it's mine," Gilbert said, "and I told him to." But there was a van at the top of the steps and it was loaded with carpet! That lot was for Charlie Bristow! Of course, he got away with it but you could hear his bones knocking! I still see that same detective in Brighton now. He's still on the railway police and he says, "Enjoy your holiday?" And of course we went on holiday to Looe the next morning. But that tickled me. And old Bert Wickham, he only had a couple of tins, you know the food tins they used to have on the cars. They had him for stealing, but he'd only taken them home to grow plants in!

Joe: Right next door to a van loaded with carpet!

Geoff: Yes, and they'd been carrying it up the stairs, too!

Don: I was sent down to Newhaven Harbour one day, to pick up the boat train coming down from London, as there was some fault on it. So I was standing there at the harbour with my bag of tools. The customs fella comes across and says, "Who are you? What are you doing here?," I said "I'm Pullman, waiting for the boat train to come in." But he looked at me a bit suspicious. He sort of kept on watching me to make sure I got on that boat train!

Geoff: And another time, I walked out of the brass shop into the main shop, and I saw everybody standing about. So I said, "What's going on here?" They said, "We're waiting for the word from Charlie," as you could take all of the carpet that was lying there. So I stood there, and then I noticed Old Chitty standing back and I thought that was funny as he's not having anything to do with this. Funny, cos he was usually first and foremost. So I took a couple of bits of green carpet. But when Chitty went out that night, he had a complete roll of new stuff!

Joe: That was the funny thing as this was literally a case of me being behind the door, as they say. I was doing something on the shop office door, down on my hands and knees in Charlie Bristow's office. When I came out, all I could see was a cloud of dust and bits of carpet going out! I wondered what was going on.

Geoff: Grabbing it left, right and centre they were!

Joe: And that was just surplus ends.

Geoff: And do you remember Bill Francis? When it was getting near Christmas time, and everyone'd be making toys, he used to stand at the end of the cars, watching. And if anyone moved, "On your toes," he'd say, and everyone stopped.

Joe: Hundreds of things they'd be. Hundreds! A lot were stuffed under the kitchens on the cars, or all over the shop! And in the workshops! You'd find little yacht lamps standing there, things like that. Little toys, and stuff like that!

Don: Another favourite trick was if the body builders were fitting the lights, you know, putting the side-lights on, and they were made of a quarter of an inch of plate glass and they had to be fitted into the mouldings on the side of the cars. So some chaps would get into a car opposite and throw tiny little screws which would hit the glass, PING, and of course, the fitters thought they'd gone and cracked the glass!

Joe: And you know those pantry cars ["buffet cars" today - NW] well, they had big arctic glass side-lights on them, and that arctic glass was pretty dodgy stuff. Same glass as they used in the kitchens. There was a chap there, pretty nervous sort of chap, Dennis something or other, working with a Lancashire bloke in one of the cars. My mate and I were in a car opposite. So we stared at him and said, "That's going to break in a minute. It's going to crack, you know." "Shut up, you silly things," he said. So of course it cracked, didn't it! What we got called when we came up the side of the car...! "Clear off, you bastards," he said. "You've put the evil eye on it!". It had cracked because he done the bolts up too tight. Those bigger bits of arctic were really dodgy.

Geoff:	Who was that chippy, the spitting image of Gilbert? Old Bill Francis went up to Gilbert thinking it was this chippy and did something and then it was Gilbert who turned round. Bill was flabbergasted!
Don:	Harold Dudeney. It was Harold Dudeney. He used to wear a blue suit, just like Old Gilbert's. One day Gilbert was bending down to tie his shoe laces. Crafty devil, old Bill, and as he went past he kneed him! It turned out it was Gilbert. Bill had to just keep walking!
Geoff:	Old Gilbert, he came up to me when the works was closing down [1963] and asked me if I'd like to work in a hospital. "Good God, no," I said. "Well what d'you want to go as?," he said. "I'd like to get a job in a bank." "My neighbour's a bank manager," he said. He came in the next day and said he'd got an appointment for me, Lloyd's Bank, Durrington. They gave me a pass to go over there, but when I went through the money, what the pay was, what the train fare worked out as, I would have been £4 a week worse off than at Pullman. I saw old Gilbert on the station and he came running up to me and asked how I'd got on. I told him I'd turned it down, because I'd have been much less well off. "But you'll get redundancy pay," he said, "it'll last you a few years". "How much is that?" I asked. "£120," he said! Well, I wrote to Barclay's and got in at North Street.
Don:	Another incident was the first Works Outings we ever had. And Gilbert he turned up in a pair of Home Guard trousers and a jacket he bought from Oxfam! When we went to Windsor. And we were all dressed up in our Sunday best. He came up and looked at us and said, "Cor, I wouldn't have recognised you."
Joe:	And he thought we'd all turn up in our works clothes!
Don:	Typical!
Geoff:	And the fighting on the coach. When we went over to Windsor. There was Charlie Hunt and Harry Dawson. They were going to set about old Ron Payne. Of course I'd only just come out of the prison service then, and I had to sort the three of them out. That quietened them down.
Don:	We went on an outing to Bournemouth once, and old Eric Cooper was there. Poor old Eric, he was crippled with multiple sclerosis, and he was about six foot five. But every time we passed another group of the Pullman, walking up the road, we'd say "Good morning". AND every time we passed them we'd keep saying "Good morning". Daft lot we were!

Geoff: A board round your neck would have been quicker!

Joe: One a year, those outings, weren't they? June or July.

Geoff: Yes, and old Frank Holman organised one, there was a committee. But it
            wasn't done through the works office. Then there used to be our cricket
            pitch, up by the old canteen. It was only a little scrap of grass, but we used
            to have a game or two on it.

Ted Brown
adds :   Then there was the angling club. Not that it was anything formal in the
            Company, just an informal get-together of people who were interested. I
            used to run that. We used to use the boats from the Southern Railway and the
            British railway clubs. 14 footers. We used to go out from Paston Place beach.
            We'd get congar eel, plaice, whiting, mackerel, dog-fish. And I used an old
            cane rod I'd won in a *News of the World* competition!

Joe: Silly times really, but there was always something happening up there!

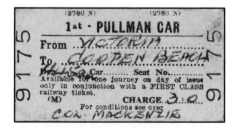

5. WOMEN WORKERS

Don: They were introduced to the works during the War. When men weren't available, and there were four or five of them, I think. There were two who worked in the trimmers shop, and they left to get married. One worked with the painters, and one with the electricians. But they still kept them on after the War, when the men were coming back. But I suppose when they got their full complement of men, the management decided to dispose of them.

Joe: But while they were at work there, they stayed their time. They weren't just sacked or ousted, or anything like that. Later on I think one was sacked and the other one was a redundancy. I suppose it must have been the late 40's.

Geoff: It was. Because I started up there in '48 and they went in '49. They used to clean lamps, things like that.

Don: And in the trimming shop, stitching up and making curtains. And with the wood machinists, lighter kind of work at the bench. But no heavy jobs on the shop floor. And I don't think they actually worked on the vehicles.

Joe: I can't recall seeing them on the cars at all. They did their work on the benches in the shop. But it wasn't awkward or anything like that, having women there. Everyone used to have a laugh, get on with each other, that sort of thing. And they joined in all the union and committee and other activities. On equal terms with the rest of us. There wasn't any second class sort of business as I recall. But what pay they got, I couldn't tell you. Then there was the cook, Mollie Batchelor, when we opened the canteen and they started to serve meals. But they were only a sort of small section, temps really.

Geoff: You mustn't forget the ones who worked in the offices. There was an office girl there, and a secretary. The girl who worked in the office, Barbara Bennett, she drove a motorbike. She could drive a 1000cc as easy as a man too.

Don: She belonged to Brighton Motorcycling Club.

Geoff: And that day when she sat in the office as you came out of the brass shop you had to pass the office and could look straight in. Old Gilbert saw the blokes running up and down there, and sent her home to change her dress. She'd got a low cut dress on. And all the blokes were dodging in and out to have a look!

Joe: And Miss Gulliland, we called her Gully, she worked in the office. One day Gilbert walked in, with Alf Reeves, the electrician with some work for her. And she had a pile of work on her desk already. And Gilbert turned to Alf and said "Give that work to Miss Gulliland. She's looking for a job." But she said, quick as a flash, "Yes, and it's not with the Pullman Car Company!" And there was Mrs. King who was up there a long time. She was one of those who'd always help other people.

Just before closure in 1963 the works staff in front of Car ARGUS (1924).

6. OUTWORK

Joe: Sometimes we'd have to go and pick up the cars as they came in to King's Cross, the 'Queen of Scots' and the 'Yorkshire Pullman'. They would come in and you would have to go up there and carry out certain jobs in those cars in traffic. You'd pick it up at King's Cross and go right up the yard with it, do what you could in the time, come back to King's Cross, and then have to fight your way through the boarding passengers. That's the way it was. It wasn't so much getting off the cars, as getting back to Brighton. You used to have to lug all sorts of stuff on the train. Then I went back on the 'Golden Arrow' to Dover seven days running. We had to fit new heaters under the basins. A hell of a job. There was over 200 of them, all the same pattern. And there was a steam pipe to be connected up. You couldn't connect up the pipes, what with all the swaying about, so what we used to do, as soon as we got to Dover, and all the time we were in Dover, we worked like stink! Then as soon as the passengers started to come back in, we packed up and came back. We'd go from Stewart's Lane early in the morning, to Victoria, back to Stewart's Lane, doing what we could before the train went out, then have a ride down to Dover, used to put us in the front compartment right next to the engine with all the exhaust from the WEST COUNTRY [Bullied 4-6-2 - Light Pacifics - NW] coming in. We'd called it the smoke hole! We'd get to Dover, the pier station, Dover Marine, really, then get stuck in for a couple of hours. One of the jobs was that the tables were coming loose, so we had to fix them. Then all the doors were sticking. This was 1951, on the new stock. We had to free the doors, do what we could in the time, and when the station pilot came to shunt us back into the station, we'd have to clear up. One day, someone opened a door, and all the shavings blew right down the train! But we couldn't do anymore after that. So back to Victoria and down to Brighton on the 'Brighton Belle' at 7.00pm I think. And we had to do all the Southern Stock, not just the Northern, but that was just running maintenance. You know, putting extra coat-hangers on. You might do a chair change in traffic. Take the side lights out, take the chairs out, change them over, then put the side lights back in. We did that on the electric cars as well. And all bits of odds and ends that could be done in traffic, we had to do. Clapham Yard, we used to go up there a lot. Changing carpets, that sort of thing. And they used to shunt like mad up Clapham Yard. You'd be trying to work, then, BANG, you'd be up the other end of the car.

Geoff: And the brass work as well. We had to carry some heavy stuff about, especially when we were doing the steptreads.

Joe: All sorts of details were done. We used to run up and down to the car sheds in Lover's Walk. Catch the cars as they came in. Perhaps you'd have an hour.

Changing hinges on the pantry door. Now round about Christmas time people would always break into the bar stock. Some crafty beggars were knocking the pin out of the hinges, taking the door off, and helping themselves. So all these hinges, they had to be welded up in the shop. There was always little jobs, silly little jobs sometimes.

Geoff: And one weekend, one Saturday and Sunday, we had to change a complete roof, up at Battersea, near the Stores. Old Alf Gee was on it with me. We used to cop quite a lot of that, changing complete roofs. One time Alf asked me to go and get a ladder out from near the dustbins. I saw them all watching me. But I went to where the dustbins were and when I went near them there were rats, as big as cats, jumping out of the bins. Honestly, I was fixed to the ground. I couldn't move! And where they used to stack the empty bottles, you could hear those bottles moving with the rats!

Don: One of those sheds use to literally move from the rats.

Geoff: Terrific size they were. And Johnny Howard was up there one day, and one of the rats jumped up his apron.

Joe: One of the young lads as he was then. Frightened the life out of him.

Geoff: Mice and that I don't take no notice of. But rats...!

Joe: Health and Safety people these days, they wouldn't allow it. And we had to do modifications as well to buildings. The offices at Victoria, on platform 17, beside the continental office. And they'd had bomb damage up there. We'd put up a temporary hut, and had to fit it out, then put partitions in the main offices, and install the furniture, office desks and so forth. And touching on those office desks, they were one of the very first jobs I got with the Pullman Company. Of course, we improvised quite a lot of those desks, typists desks, from material recovered from the canteen car counters and fittings that had been used for the NAFFI trains, the troop trains. We also used a lot of plywood sheets that had been used as blackout in the electric cars running in the early days of the War. As timber was in short supply, everything had to be used economically. I fell in for a lot of that work. But it was bench work, and I enjoyed that as it was my line. They were done in the workshop, those desks, and then sent up in the 'Brighton Belle', for Victoria and places like that, and the Mayfair Place office. But the main offices, the general offices for the staff superintendent, catering superintendent and so forth, were all at Victoria, just off Platform 1. There was another office, right out at the end of what was Platform 19. We did occasional jobs in there. And we did a lot of work at Battersea, altering counters and things like that, counters for the food preparation department. And for the loading department, putting shelves up, stuff like that. This wasn't piece-work. No, we got paid the hourly rate, and overtime. We got paid overtime, if we had to leave early from Brighton Station, and we got free travel of course. We used to take a sidings pass out. We got that from our office in Brighton. That covered you for travel all over the central section. And we used the same pass for Folkestone, as I recall.

Don: I went to Dover on the 'Golden Arrow' on a pass like that.

Geoff: Yes, and I had to as well.

Don: And if we could, we'd do the job in traffic. Mostly we had to wait until the train stopped and then go like the clappers. We couldn't do much, because of the vibrations. We had three little sink heaters, which had to be changed. We did one a day until they were finished. We had to go from Brighton to Victoria, then down to Folkestone and Dover Marine. One day, Friday, when we were working on the 'Golden Arrow' fitting these heaters under the washbasins, I said to my mate, Frank Campbell, that instead of waiting to go back to Victoria on the boat train we could go down to Dover Priory station and then along the coast. And of course we were home a damn sight later than if we'd gone back up to Victoria! We had to change at Ashford, then at Hastings. He called me everything, he did!

Joe: There were other outside jobs too. I used to have to go solo to Ore sheds, at Hastings, sometimes in the electric cars, riding out and back. But I got called out for a job, by myself, at Hastings station itself. There was a little cupboard under the main stairway on the down platform, used by the car's staff and where some of the stuff was stored. And the door-lock had broken somehow. I had to force my way in, put a new lock on and get it to work, and then I went and locked myself out! I was stuck out there on the platform in my apron! I had to borrow a bar from somewhere, force the lock, and then go and buy another lock! Luckily it was fine weather. Then there was another strange place we had to go to. There was an office in Stratton Street, Mayfair. It was only a small office, I think, and I had to walk across Hyde Park. But from the ridiculous to the sublime, one of the classiest jobs we ever got, and Wally Verrall was on it with me, was the Shareholders Meeting Room at Euston Station. There was an exhibition being prepared there, called "The Royal Journey". We had to install a mock-up of a half section of a Victorian car, with a coupé. And we had to be very careful where we walked, and what we put down, as the floor had been just highly polished. The place had just been restored to its former splendour. And Mr Scholes, he became curator of Clapham Museum [now closed and its exhibits transferred to national collection at York Railway Museum - NW], was in charge of that job. That was a most unusual job, that was. And another funny job I had to do was to fit torpedo ventilators to the Store Shed on Brighton number 1 platform. They are still there to this day! Another place we had to visit on occasions to pick up cars was Streatham. Very often cars that were out of traffic were stored down there. Then they were sent round from there to Battersea sheds or to Stewart's Lane, where they were commissioned again. We did jobs up there, freeing doors, stopping doors from rattling, packing luggage racks forward. Two of us had to do that one day as we were riding in the cars from Eardley Sidings to Stewart's Lane, Herne Hill, Tulse Hill that way. Then we'd have to get the cars from the Eastern Region down to Brighton. But only a few of them were allowed through the Metropolitan. There were two ways they could come, down the spur from Finsbury Park to Canonbury. Then they'd have to reverse back over the top of Willesden Junction, then round the West London Line to Clapham Junction and down that way. But some could go via the Snow Hill Tunnel [now used by Thameslink Bedford - Brighton trains - NW]. But that was gauge restricted. The big twelve-wheel cars could not use that way. And at one time there were a lot of twelve-wheelers in service. Some actually came off the old Great Eastern Railway. But Clapham Yard was an awkward place to work. We often got jobs there. We would wait for a car to come off a boat train, up to Waterloo, unload and then come back down again. There were plenty of them in those days, mostly from Southampton. When you were there, you'd find you might have to walk all the way down to Wandsworth Town Station because it was a very long siding. It was a long way to walk with a bag of tools and a table top, a damn long walk on a hot day, carrying all your stuff!

Geoff: A shunter was killed up Battersea one day. The train was shunting and he got jammed between the buffers.

Joe: That isn't surprising, what used to go on up there! And talking about rough shunts, there was one in Lover's Walk shed once. It was one of the electric cars, and the train had been split, leaving the car at the South End. And the train was putting back and the chap thought he had a six car train, but he had a twelve. So he knocked that car right over the concrete stop-block there. Stripped all the undergear right out of that car!

Don: Then there was the occasion when during the night they pushed a train up the wash road past the Pullman, and the driver pushed it right over the path nearly down into the spur and broke the gas-pipe.

46

Joe: The gas mains for the Pullman used to go behind those buffers and it cut it all off.

Don: The driver was down the Brighton end...

Joe: He thought he had a six car too, but he had a twelve so he went through the buffers. It took two tank engines to pull that car out. The last place that I can think of which we used to get to for traffic jobs was Finsbury Park Yard. That was on the up side of the line, north of Finsbury Park Yard. Might be still there for all I know! [It is - NW!]. There was no shed there, just open sidings. 'Tyne-Tees' and 'Yorkshire Pullman' we used to get there, doing little jobs on them while we were shunted over the flying junction to the down side!

Electricians gang in front of one of the Devon Belle observation cars.

7. OF TITLED TRAINS AND SPECIAL CARS

Joe: The 'Golden Arrow' used to run down to Folkestone Harbour, and to Dover Marine at some times, and the Ostend Boat Train. Not the 'Thanet Belle' though, that was to Margate and Ramsgate [From 1951-1958, when withdrawn, this was called the 'Kentish Belle' - NW]

Don: Those 'Thanet Belle' cars were originally hospital cars during the First World War, I believe, converted to Pullmans.

Joe: Old cars on the 'Thanet Belle' mainly. Mostly ex-London and North Western Railway, but there was an odd Great Western vehicle among them. And I think there was a Lancashire and Yorkshire Railway one as well, but I couldn't be sure. [Both the London and North Western Railway and the Lancashire and Yorkshire Railway ceased to exist in 1923! - NW]. Original frames but new bodies on them. And because they were ex-ambulance cars they were very soft sprung. And there was one in the shop under the gantry, in for repairs or something. And you could rock one of those cars with one hand, or by just putting your foot on it. Much to the annoyance of anyone working inside! The 'Golden Arrow' had a bit of a struggle from Folkestone Harbour, had to have three or four tank engines on to help it get up the bank, but we didn't have to do any modifications for clearance on those cars. The only ones I know were modified, and that was before my time, were two of the old 'Southern Belle' cars, MYRTLE and GROSVENOR. They had their roofs lowered, I believe.

Don: Yes, I believe they did. They were too high.

Joe: They used to run from Brighton to Newhaven, but it was something to do with the Bo-Peep tunnel at Hastings.

Don: There was an occasion when MYRTLE and GROSVENOR had to be taken from the works up to London. Somehow they got made up into a train going through the Bo-Peep tunnel. When they went through the tunnel, the ventilators on the side of the roof got knocked off. Our department had to cut them down and put a strip of copper over the top to make it last.

Joe: Of course the ones that weren't gauge-restricted, could go anywhere, were the little Hastings cars [Built 1926, taken into Southern Region stock 1958, withdrawn by 1963, usually painted green - NW]. And to catch those in traffic you had to go to a place called Rotherhithe Road, by South Bermondsey

Station. I had two or three trips on those. And one of those Hastings cars has been preserved. It's on the Kent and East Sussex Railway, BARBARA. The six cars were CAMILLA, THEODORA, LATONA, MADELINE, BARBARA and PAMONA.

Don: Incidentally, GROSVENOR and MYRTLE were the heaviest vehicles we had, apart from the 'Brighton Belle' power cars. 42 tons they were.

Geoff: What were those cars built at our works? Ted Browning, Ernie Sweetman and Alf Gee, they had one each.

Joe: CYGNUS, PHOENIX, and CARINA.

Geoff: CARINA was one of them. Because old Frank Roach came down from Lancing to work on it. And he had to lower the crane down to the bogie. And he put an egg onto the bolt where it went into the bogie. And I thought, "Blimey, there won't be much of that egg left!" But he stopped the crane, just as it was resting on the egg! He didn't even crack it!

Joe: PHOENIX has an interesting story. She did literally rise from the ashes! She burnt right down to the underframes at Micheldever Station [1936 - NW]. She was originally RAINBOW. Re-built on a second-hand underframe as well. Then we had to do the 'Devon Belle' Observation cars, two of them. The engineer in charge in London, Mr Sedcole, had just died, and all the work just fell on Gilbert and our drawing office chaps. They more or less got the company out of trouble, and to their credit, they did a good job, even if a lot of it had to be made up as they went along! [The two 'Devon Belle' observation cars were originally London and North Western Railway ambulance cars in 1918, converted to Pullman in 1921, re-built as bar-cars in 1937, and then as the two observation cars 13 and 14 for the 'Devon Belle' - 1951-1953. 13 has gone to The Torbay Railway and 14 has ended up in California, both being preserved - NW].

49

8. ACCIDENTS AND INCIDENTS

Don: One day Smithers had to take the panelling in front of a washbasin down and found a notice in front of him in big bold letters. "660 VOLTS" it said. Well that was enough to scare the living daylights out of old Smithers. So he went and saw the railway about it. And the railway chap went underneath, and found the main switch or contact or something. So he turned it off and hung a napkin from the vehicle over it, so everyone could see it had been taken out of service. Then after lunch, Gilbert went down with old Smithers and us. Then Smithers noticed the napkin had been taken off the vehicle, and there was no way he was going to work on that vehicle until somebody had come and checked it!

Geoff: Another day they were burning off under the gantry. There was a bit of a hue and cry, as they'd gone and caught the coach on fire!

Don: And there was another fire in the wood machine shop caused by some sawdust getting under the planer. It got mixed up with some oil from the machinery and there was a combustion from the old electrical fittings. They were really old fashioned. There were great big blocks of wood over them and somehow the flames licked up and burnt them. Fortunately it never got as far up as the roof. But when they came in in the morning, they touched the planer and it was still warm. The fire had burnt itself out. It just happened to be lucky that nobody had stood bits of wood round it.

Joe: Or shavings. There was a fire in the shop one day, a dull afternoon. I was near Jack Butler's bench at the time and had just gone to the toilet. And there was a hullabaloo near REGINA, one of those old wooden cars, oak-pannelled. They were stripping down the inside, and the bloke doing the stripping had gone home, when the paint stripper caught fire. Charlie Bristow jumped in, he went into the coupé, and I saw him go down. Someone went in and got him out. It was the fumes from the stripper had got to him. He had to go to hospital.

Don: That was the French Polishers stripping out a saloon. It was winter and pretty cold. Someone had got one of those electric heaters in the saloon which wasn't being stripped and unfortunately the fumes met up with the fire. I was down the bottom of the shop with Charlie Bristow and he suddenly said, "Someone has set the car on fire!" I looked up the shop and there was all flames coming out of a window, Ben Farr managed to jump out onto a plank outside. I went haring down the shop to get the fire extinguisher, the full length of the shop nearly, and had just started to run back with it when someone shouted, "It's all right, it's out". And of course it was mainly the paint-stripper that was burning rather than the car. Then another time this chap came down the works, he'd been a conductor on the Southdown Buses and he'd got the sack because he'd kidded the driver into letting him reverse the bus and he'd had an accident. He came to the Pullman as a labourer. Now at the back of the guard's brake on the cars, there was steps up there, on the steel cars that was. Well of course he wouldn't use a ladder. He had to be clever and climb up these steps, and his hand lost its grip at the top and down he went. He had a pot of white paint to paint the wall and that fell all over him! We had to drag him out of the pit and take him up the hospital, but I don't think he did himself a lot of damage.

Geoff: What about Freddie Mills? He stepped onto the live rail, on the Highcroft Villas side, and got badly burnt. He was off for a long time.

Joe: Yes, that was a very dangerous spot, and it still is. If you've got to walk down from the shop to the car sheds at Lover's Walk, you've got to cross one of the running roads, well, a siding, the washer road or the other, the outer straight. And that was the most dangerous spot of the lot. You had to pick your spot very carefully, and watch what you were carrying that it didn't trail on the live rail. Bert Hill nearly brought it down there one day. He was taking one of those long brass grab bars down with him and it was waving about, so I had to shout at him to pick it up or he'd get sparks!

Geoff: Ted Phillips went down the sheds once as he was taking off a step and you know those steps had a brass rail. As he was taking the rail off he dropped it. So he went to grab it and it touched the live rail and it shook him like a dog shaking a rat! But the thing that used to tickle me was in the mornings seeing the platelayers working on the spur. Suddenly they'd sit down on the live rail!

Don: Only when it was dry!

Joe: You'd treat that with great respect. Two things, a pane of glass and the live rail, you'd treat with the greatest respect. Treat them properly, and they'd be kind to you. Play tricks with them and they'll get their own back.

Geoff: But it tickled me that time. I saw three of them there, the ganger and two other guys. I said to George, "Blimey, they're going to commit suicide!" Three of them just sitting on the live rail!

51

Don:	You know there was always a pipe under the bowl of the toilet, the soil pipe. And it was blocked with ice one day. And old Fred Clayton says to me, "Get over here with your blow lamp." And the driver was sitting in the cab, ready to take the train out! "You must be mad," I said, "I'm not going under there!" There was another little incident one day, before the war. A kitchen car had been brought in, and we was ordered to strip it out completely as there were beetles on this car. I don't know whether someone'd had a beetle served up with their lunch or what. But there was a definite panic on. So we stripped it out, and someone got one of these beetles, so he sent it away for analysis. And the verdict came back that it was a "bacon beetle."
Joe:	Yes, that's right, a "bacon beetle".
Don:	And this became a sort of standing joke, you know. "Look out for the bacon beetles behind you," someone would shout. It was a hell of a job when we had to do a complete strip out on those vehicles. It wasn't just hardboard. It was tongue-and-grooved. We had to take out partitions, and go up in all the little nooks and crannies with a blow-lamp, making sure there were none in there. Then they had to stuff it full of vermicene. And spray it. Every vehicle that came in at that time, had to be stripped right down, all the insulation from behind the stove, all had to be completely gutted. I reckon someone must have had a "bacon beetle" in their food! And they kept that up for some time. Every kitchen vehicle was stripped down. All the asbestos and sheeting behind the stove was ripped off and all the kitchen fittings taken out. Then always a thorough delousing, then everything put back. While the panic reigned, that was. Then it all died down.
Geoff:	And can you remember old Harding coming down saying it was costing the company thousands of pounds where women were getting into the cars and tearing their stockings on the chairs.
Don:	Or claiming they were!
Joe:	The only time I saw woodworm on a car, I can't remember which one it was now, was in one of those finishing panels. It was literally alive with them! One of those polished finishing panels. And you looked at it, and the woodworm were emerging right in front of you. Just that one particular car, and that one particular panel.
Don:	We had a vehicle brought in one day because there was a rat on it. It had evidently got in on a siding somewhere and it had made its nest at the back of one of the armchairs, in the padding and stuff.

Joe:	Can't have been used very much.

Don: Anyway, they opened this vehicle up, and a crowd of fellas stood round with sticks and they were going to thump this rat when it came out. But the rat was too fast for them, it got away.

Joe: Talking about livestock, one day Ernie Allen and myself, and I think Wally Verrall was there as well but I can't be too sure, had to go and pick up a car that had been knocked out of traffic. She was Stewart's Lane car shed. And the ice-chest had still got all the food in it. Now that car had been out there a few hot days. So when we opened the ice-box door, there was a whole steady stream of maggots fall out of that. The only thing we could do was sweep it all out and disinfect it. One of those old 'Kentish Belle' cars if I remember rightly.

Don: Then you might get a vehicle taken out of traffic because the railway said it had got a hot-box or something. Of course the attendant didn't know until he was told his car was being taken out of traffic. Then it would stand on a siding for a few days and if you went on the vehicle and opened the ice-box then you'd find sardines with a coat of fur on them!

Joe: Then there was another incident. It fell to Harry Yeates. He was drilling through the steel end of one of the composite cars to fit the luggage grid [to protect the panels from accidental damage by luggage - NW]. Drilled right through the panel, the emergency brake-pipe, the passenger alarm one, that is. This was on a Friday so over the weekend the car was shunted out and coupled in its unit. The motor-man came on the Monday to try and "make his brake", to test his brakes, but could not get his pressure up. He was able to trace it back to the emergency brake pipe. So the car had to be taken out of traffic, not that it ever went in really, so it wasn't a danger or anything. The whole of the small pantry had to be completely stripped, wood an' all, to get to the pipe. So one little hole, no more than 5/16ths, made a hell of a lot of work!

53

9. VISITING ENGINES, SHUNTERS AND SHUNTING

Joe:
The little BRIGHTON TERRIER came in one day. They'd already cleaned her up and handed her over to the preservation people. That was the Lancing Works shunter 680S. But she was bits of other engines as well when she went out. Half the original also made up of bits from the other works shunter 377S. It was cannibalised. It's now known as WADDON. Went to London as a static exhibit. But ended up in Canada now. But she was a Brighton engine originally. But sold to the South Eastern Railway. Spent most of her life there, so she had a lot of South Eastern fittings on her. But ended her working life at Lancing. And the best thing I ever saw that little works shunter, 377S, do, was to pull three of those War Department 2-8-0s which were being brought back from overseas. I hadn't been at the Pullman long and there were three of them in the top yard [opposite the Preston Park Works - NW] on the down side of the line. We were sitting out one lunchtime, me and my mate, when she came tootling up the line. I said, "Look at this. I bet she's come up for those 2-8-0s. She'll take them one at a time." Well, the fireman got up on the tender, to take the tender brakes off, and she took the lot away with her. No fuss at all! Mind you, there's a bit of a falling grade there. Yes, she just took the three heavy engines away with her and you could have lost her in one of their tenders. And she had been at the front, you wouldn't have been able to see her. And there were two of the old D1 0-4-2 tanks at Brighton then. 252 and 253. 252 was BUCKHURST and the 253 was PELHAM. And once or twice in the early days just after I started one of these would come up to shunt at Preston Park. To do the morning shunting, and little 253 would move half the 'Brighton Belle'. And she was about 70 years old by then! And in Lancing Yard, when we were working there once, I saw a little terrier move a whole electric unit, and you know what they weighed [probably something like 250 tons - NW]. You see that was the interesting bit, you never knew what was going to turn up on the yard. Most times you had the same engine, but turn your back and something different, unusual, would turn up. They used to come up, of course, from Brighton Sheds. The regular one was an 0-4-4, a D3 bogie tank. For a heck of a long time too. It used to do a trip out to Sheffield Park, shunt the Brighton Abattoir sidings at Lewes Road, staying out there until she was required up the Pullman Yard. But we would get anything up there at times. Used to get a South Eastern D 4-4-0 tender loco at times. And that was an awful engine to shunt with. And very often the South Eastern H 0-4-4 tanks. Later on the M7s were regular, including 30053 the one now preserved at Swanage. You used to get sick of the sight of her! And 0-6-2 tanks, the Brighton E4 radials and a K 2-6-0 occasionally. And the I3 4-4-2 tanks were up there. And the last of the I1Xs,

one or two times, 2002, a splendid engine! But the I3 wasn't a good engine to shunt with, her wheels were too high, considering the shunting operations, bringing new cars in, finished ones out, changing vehicles to different roads, putting cars into the gantry.

Don: Incidentally, at one time the wagon busters used to do their wagon busting in that yard. They used to repair their wagons right in front of the Pullman! I always remember the wagon busters, as they had an old railway vehicle out there, a sort of carriage base, where they'd get out of the rain and make themselves a cup of tea. When the rain was really hard they'd get in there but when the sun shone, they used to get out and work like the clappers because they were paid piecework. I said to Fred that if they picked up four shillings a week they were lucky. That was before the War tho'.

Joe: Talking of shunting I've got to mention Ted Phillips. He was on the underframe gang in the shop, known as the heavy gang, and he was a chargehand. So he always used to supervise the shunting. He only had one call! He'd shout, "Hold tight on Five!" irrespective of which road the car would be coming in on. So when you heard that, you just had to work it out! You just had to take cover!

Don: I remember the building before they had the steel shutters. There were big wooden doors, and one day a truck came flying through those doors, and there was a car up on the stocks. And you know those big trestles, well, someone threw one of those in the way of the truck to stop it. Otherwise the car would have been a write-off.

Joe: Then there was the occasion when two cars ran away as they were going out. Chaps were in them, too. SHEILA was one, but I can't remember the other. And they went right down to the buffers in the electric car sheds. Didn't do the buffers much good, or the cars either!

Don: I remember several coming off at the points. You see when they pulled them out into the yard, there was no way they could brake them. They should have been blocked. But they pulled them out and left them standing there. And trains would come by at some point, and what with the vibration they'd move off! So there were times when the work's been going a bit behind like, and somebody's had to go out to do a bit of finishing off and they'd find the car gone!

Joe: One of the strangest jobs I did in that yard, and I hadn't been there all that long, was that I had to start stripping a car. It was LORRAINE, one of those

that had been in store on the Eastern Region. A steel car she was. She'd not been in traffic, but she was coming in for an overhaul. I opened the lock, and dropped the end ceiling. And it was a solid mass of flies! So if you want to know where flies go in winter, they go into a Pullman car!

Don: Talking about that shunting yard, there used to be a fella out there, he eventually took over the brakedown gang. Fellow named Scrace, strong as an ox, and he stuttered really badly. Sometimes when they were lowering things under these wagons, instead of getting blocks or jacks to take the weight, Scrace would bend down there and take the weight of it on his back, then crawl along with it and another fellow would take it off him. Well you know what those blokes are! One day they wouldn't take it off, and poor old Scrace was stuck fast!

[There was no live rail laid into the Pullman works so all shunting had to be undertaken by steam locomotives until the works closed in 1963 - NW]

Opposite: BR 32646, built in 1876, now preserved as FRESHWATER on the Isle of Wight railway, seen here shunting at Preston Park with car AURELIA on 5th April 1963. L. to R. Mr. Gilbert, the Works Manager, Mr. Bristow, the Works Foreman, Mr. Johnson, the Works Engineer.
Above: Visitors from British Railways: a driver, fireman and two shunters drop in. Top right is Ernie Smith, Harry Dawson in shirt sleeves, Ted Phillips (hatless), Tom Vinall on an oil gas tank wagon, 10th May 1950.

10. WORKSHOP COMMITTEES

Joe: In the workshop committee we did get some safety measures through that were outstanding. Shunting was carried out in the body shop, and there was nothing on the end of those roads to prevent a car taking right off. So they gave us stop blocks. Also outside the shop, there were a set of rail stubs set in the ground with a sleeper, or a heavy timber, on a loose chain across them, which protected the shop from anything coming into it. But it was best to be out the way when anything was shunting. There was a shop fund for all this. A penny a week was the regular fee. Nobody ever complained about that, as far as I can recall. It was to pay for the Shop Steward, or any other union business. There were regular meetings of the committee.

Don: It was once a month, wasn't it.

Joe: Yes, we'd meet amongst ourselves, and then we met management. Usually Gilbert, the works manager. There certainly used to be some interesting discussion on it. And it wasn't a waste of time. It was taken seriously. It wasn't just a free-for-all chin-wag or anything. Safety measures, that was the main thing, if the lighting was poor, protection, or if the steps to Highcroft Villas got a bit dangerous. I doubt if it's still there but outside the main door, there was a rail put up between the edge of the path and the railway line, the spur line. That was because everybody used to pour out of that door once they had clocked off, and there were youngsters there as well, so there was a risk of people falling on the line or in front of a train.

Don: Or the roof, when the glass panes needed fixing, or painting over in summer.

Joe: That was a regular rainmaker that was! Every year when the summer came round, they used to whitewash the glass. So of course when they'd done it, bad weather would set in immediately! But the committee would take any little grumbles the shop floor would come up with, and bring them up at the next meeting. It wasn't strictly a union committee, because I shouldn't have been on it. I wasn't in the Vehicle Builders Union. I was in the carpenters. And there were electricians on it too. And plumbers, trimmers, coach-builders, painters and so forth. It was a big shop committee, that was all.

Don: Were the wood-machinists on it?

Joe: No, I don't think they were. There were five or six people on it. There were three distinct gangs in the body shop, each with a chargehand, but one used

The guy with Ray Monk, Les Greenow, Harry Lamper, Ernie Wenham, Idris Edwards, Roy Clements.

to represent the lot. I used to scribble things in a little notebook, then bring it out at the next meeting to see if it was worth taking to management, or whether we'd settle it ourselves. But there were a lot of things that were achieved through it.

Don: And then there was a canteen committee at one time. But the management eventually shut it down as they thought it a bit of a waste. There were too many people running it than what there was working! But it only ran for about two or three years.

Joe: Of course it was useful, and it took up quite a bit of time, when the canteen was being proposed. DEVONSHIRE [b.1904 - NW] had got into a state, ready for scrapping. The new one was built on brick piers. Then they got some tie-bars second-hand from Lancing Works, or from someone on the carriages, and then the section above was built on top of that. Then parts of ALBERT EDWARD [b.1877], glass and panels and stuff like that was used in the kitchen. The north end was partitioned off for the stove and kitchen facilities.

Don: VERONA, one of the old 'Southern Belle' cars, was used for that.

Joe: It was where the timber store cage was, adjacent to the end door and the mill doors.

Geoff: And don't forget the Benevolent Fund.

Joe: Yes, we had raffles, mostly run for the Benevolent Fund. Usually on a Friday afternoons, but sometimes Mondays and Fridays. Mainly chocolates, or small sums of money, but we had meat on it as well. Whoever used to run it would put the numbers in a drum, a shop-made drum, and give it a turn. The plumbers came out of it quite well, I seem to remember.

Don: It was all done fair and square, all above board!

Joe: Yes, there was no fiddle to it, it was run on straight lines and there were only modest amounts of money. Sixpence or a shilling. But as luck would have it, you used to get a run of the same people winning it every week. There was a chap called Bill Winton, old chap, retired from the railway. He was a sort of shop labourer and he won about six or seven weeks running at a time.

Don: He used to stoke the boiler as though he were trying to make it move up to Preston Park station!

Joe: He was an ex-engine driver, used to drive a 'Brighton Atlantic'. Then there was another chap, one of the railway firemen. He used to make a practice of coming up to supervise the fire precautions. That was his excuse, I think, because he used to come up and have a go on the raffle. He had quite a run on it too. I can't remember his name now. It used to be quite a laugh. Then there were other raffles or sweepstakes they used to have on Derby Day or other big races. I won that twice as it happens! Picked up a few things. And I won the raffle once. It was all part of the scene. But it all went to the Benevolent Fund. This would pay out for any fella who was off sick, or had to lose time for some reason. Only if we thought it was a deserving case, you know. The Fund was administered through the committee.

Don: Wasn't there a Benevolent Fund Committee?

Joe: Yes, there was. Stan Cobbett dealt with that. But it was a very good thing. I couldn't work one time. I was off work for two or three weeks. And Jim Humphries came up one night and brought me a donation from it.

Pullman Works Kitchen car. Ex ALBERT EDWARD, assembled Derby 1877 from American built parts showing the origional American with clerestory. Later converted to third class car No 4. The white end housed the kitchen. Photographed in the late 40's

11. LOST AND FOUND

Joe:
The stuff we used to find in the cars! The most amazing thing was Alf Gee, one of the chargehands, and that great big pistol! Suddenly he appeared in one of the side-lights of the car, when they'd been taken out, appeared brandishing this darn great wild-western pistol! He found it in a toilet cupboard. Everybody, of course everybody, just scattered while he was waving this thing around. We nipped off down the scaffold, smartish.

Don:
One day Charlie Bristow came out of the office and said that someone had to go down to the Brighton Belle as a man'd dropped a gold cigarette case down the toilet. So Dick Cosham went down. When he got down there, there was a queue of people, railwaymen, cleaners all stretching out from this toilet. And a man said to him, "Have you come down to get my cigarette case?" "It would make a change if I could get in there!" Dick replied! It appeared that this gold cigarette case had been down there for three of four days. And of course everybody was keeping quiet in the hope they would find this case. Now the usual railway toilets went straight out onto the track. So the attendants has told this fella, "Oh, you won't see that again. It's probably fallen through and got smashed up by now." But they knew full well that Pullman car toilets had a trap on them and it would be in there. Anyway, Dick couldn't do anything then as it was on the 'Belle' and it was due to go out. But he picked the 'Belle' up again about 4 o'clock so I said, "Well, take the pan out, and lock the toilet up when you've finished until such time as we can get it put back." So Dick goes down there, gets the pan out and finds the cigarette case in all the muck! He brings it back up the Pullman. "Put it in a bucket of disinfectant," I said. And when they opened it the cigarettes were still in there, but of course nobody wanted them! Then he handed the case over to Charlie Bristow. "You want to watch him with that cigarette case," I said, "If there's any reward to come it's yours, because you did all the dirty work." A couple of days later, he asked Charlie about the case, he said he'd forgotten to send it down. Then another day went by, and I asked him, because I was in charge of plumbing then, and he said, "No, I'll send it down to Brighton Station." Well somebody went down with a packet, whether it was the cigarette case, I don't know, but we heard no more about it. Maybe the police at the station had it, or even Charlie himself. We never heard, there was no reward or nothing.

Geoff:
It used to tickle me when they was stripping the cars out, and painters and labourers would be standing round. "What are they standing round for?" I asked Bert. "You watch 'em," he said, and true enough as soon as he took the carpets up there they was looking for money!

Joe: That was known as ratting. When you used to strip the seats out, you would often find coins and things lodged under a rail or down the side of the seats. Only small change tho'. And plenty of foreign coins. I've still got a little penknife at home I found under one of the seats. God knows whose it was!

Don: Sometimes half the backing of the seats would be gone, even before the vehicle got in the works!

Joe: And another little trick was to give the first class armchairs a bit of a shove, and if there was a rattle then you knew you'd got a coin down there! Or you lifted the seat to see if anything fell out.

Joe: Nothing of value was found.

Don: There was another occasion, I don't know what service it was on, when a woman got out with a plastic handbag. She put the handbag down beside her but, unfortunately, there was a steam leak on the radiator. So when she went to pick her handbag up, all she had got was the handle! So goodbye to her plastic handbag!

Joe: One interesting thing I did salvage, and it was on a kitchen car if I remember, was a small bag full of supplementary tickets. I've still got some of them. Collector's items, now I should think [yes! - NW].

12. OUTINGS AND TRIPS

Joe: We had an outing to Wilton once, I remember. But I think it was a special trip, rather than a works outing. It was for the people who'd worked on the 'Devon Belle', because it had been fitted out with Wilton carpets. There were two trips, I believe. I went on one with Alf Clayton, I think. You just had a trip from Waterloo to Wilton, where they changed engines, so there was just time to have a look round the place before you came back again.

Don: Then we had one to Bournemouth, and wasn't there one to the Isle of Wight?

Joe: Yes, there was, but I didn't go on that one. I think that one was where they used a 'Brighton Belle' unit to Portsmouth. Most unusual to see a 'Belle' unit on the coast line in those days.

Don: And later on, of course, the scope for choice for outings by train became a bit more limited. Because the railway would put a coach for us on the back of a train, but places to go became a bit fewer! So we had to hire coaches.

Joe: That was my first trip, a coach out to Windsor, 1947 or '48 I should think.

Don: I know we went to Southend once. I could tell you something about that Southend trip, but I don't think I ought to! Then we went on a football outing once, to see Brighton play Crystal Palace. It snowed hard, I think.

Geoff: Yes, it snowed so hard the match had to be abandoned. And old Harty, he took us round his house, bought three or four pounds of fish which we was eating in relays, and suddenly there was a dart flying across the table. They was playing darts!

Don: He was a pantomime he was, a proper cockney. He went into this fish shop and said to the fella, "Put some 'addock on the scales!", so the fella puts a couple of pieces on. "No, more than that," says Harty. And I said, "No we can't all go round to his place, it's not reasonable." It was just after the War, see, when things were a bit tight. But that didn't affect old Harty! So we all finished up playing cards round his place at the end. And we had several kids there and there was money being dropped on the floor, and the kids were all scrabbling around for it. So after we'd finished up the boys had a whip-round for the kids. They did quite well out of that.

Geoff:	He was a glazier, Harty. Had his own business, you know. Doing the coloured glass in churches, and that. They all came down to Brighton on an outing one day, from their pub up Crystal Palace. So they went along the seafront and we was watching them. The Salvation Army was down there and they was joining in with them, but there was a couple of yobos down there, taking the mickey! They just went at them, rattled their heads together and threw them in the sea! They never had a good coach to come down in, just one of those old fashioned ones, solid tyres and all. You should have seen them coming up the Circus! My brother-in law, George, he worked with them during the War. Used to go night watching, the ARP. They were at Marks and Spencer in Croydon, and when they came off in the morning, they had enough sugar on them to last twelve months!
Don:	He was a typical cockney, a good hearted bloke. Looked after his wife and family. They came first. When he got paid his first consideration was if his wife wanted anything, or the kids.
Geoff:	She'd had six kids, but to look at her, you wouldn't think she'd been married ten minutes. Thin as a rake!
Joe:	Then we went on an outing to Folkestone once, to look round the train ferry dock. And because there was an unusual shunting engine there. We looked round the trains, the pumping equipment, too see how everything was operated. And we went on the ferry itself, the 'Shepperton'. That was a proper works outing, organised by the railway of course. In Pullman cars attached to an ordinary train. It was all very well organised. We went to London Bridge by train, had breakfast on the train, tables were set up on the ordinary stock, got out at London Bridge and then to the ordinary service train with a couple of Pullman cars attached to the rear for our men. We had a twelve-wheeler, I can't remember the name, an old timber-bodied twelve-wheeler, a lovely smooth ride that was. So down to the sidings at Dover where we had dinner in the train. Then we went off down into the town on our own devices. And Dick Cosham was looking for tropical fish, as I remember, it was his hobby. Then back to Folkestone Central where we picked up the train to Charing Cross this time, then back home again. A lovely day.

AFTERWORD

"IT'S NOT PULLMAN"

"It's not Pullman" was one of the sayings of Mr Gilbert, the Works Manager. It was of course shorthand for a great many things, but it can stand as testimony to the very high standards of craftsmanship that existed in the Pullman Car Company's works at Preston Park, testimony that is borne out by the workers themselves whose reminiscences I have been fortunate to share. When I was recording their memories I was struck not only by that craftsmanship but the respect they held for other craftsmen. But there was more than just craftsmanship at the Pullman. The words of Joe Kent "You didn't make life difficult for your mates," show the comradeship and cooperation that existed there. The men seemed to know their own jobs, got on with them, and respected the same qualities in their work-mates. Nobody poached on anybody else's craft. And although there was the traditional, for those times, hierarchical management structure, using the armed services as a model, there was a very high degree of self management and "sorting it out between ourselves." Of course reminders were needed now and then, as another of Mr. Gilbert's pronouncements reveals. "Your treating this car worse than a garden shed," he would say when the workmanship didn't reach his exacting standards. And considering the working conditions which seemed to border on chaos at times, the workmanship did meet those exacting standards. Morale was high, not only as these reminiscences show, but also as the very low accident rate, given the potentiality for accidents in a heavy engineering workshop, reveals. And again, it wasn't only craftsmanship of a very high order, but design as well. "Old ladies and small children have got to use the cars." Mr. Gilbert again, a lesson that was not lost on the men and women at Preston Park, but does appear to be lost on the designers of British Rail's latest passenger stock.

I very much enjoyed recording and editing the reminiscences of Don Carter, Geoff Hart and Joe Kent. I hope you have enjoyed reading them. And I hope this book stands as some sort of tribute to an actual working community in Brighton from 1946 to 1963.

Nick Wellings,
Brighton.

SELECT BIBLIOGRAPHY

If you'd like to know more about Pullman operations and cars, you might like to have a look at:

Behrend, George, *Pullman in Europe*, Ian Allen 1962.

Burt and Beckerlegg, *Pullman and Perfection*, Ian Allen, 1948.

Hamilton Ellis, C., *London, Brighton and South Coast Railway*, Ian Allen 1971.

Haresnape, Brian, *Pullman: Travelling in Style*, Ian Allen 1987.

Kidner, R. W., *Pullman Cars on the "Southern"*, Oakwood Press 1987.

Morell, Julian, *Pullman*, David and Charles 1983.

Owen, N., *The Brighton Belle*, Southern Electric Group 1981.

There is also a Pullman Society, membership enquiries to Ray Addy, 42, Berkeley Street, Leeds, LS8 3RW.

The Pullman Car Company had a long and successful working relationship with the London, Brighton and South Coast Railway. For further information on this contact The Brighton Circle, membership enquiries to Brian Quemby, 67, St. Peter's Street, South Croydon, CR2 7DG.

GLOSSARY

ARCTIC GLASS:	frosted glass, rather brittle, used in lavatory windows.
BRICK PIERS:	specially constructed one-off brick columns for the temporary support of heavy weights.
BRIGHTON ATLANTIC:	a famous class of locomotive with the 4-4-2 wheel formation ("Atlantic") used for the best trains on the London Brighton and South Coast Railway from 1905 until the last one, BEACHY HEAD, was withdrawn by British Railways in 1953.
BRIGHTON TERRIER:	another famous design of the London Brighton and South Coast Railway. There were 0-6-0 wheel arrangement shunting engines designed by William Stroudly from 1872 onwards. Several can still be seen on preserved railway lines.
BOGIE:	a truck of two or more pairs of wheels used to carry the Pullman Cars.
CAMBER:	a tilt or leaning to compensate for movement.
CAR(S):	Pullmans were never called carriages but "cars" only.
CHOKER:	a muffler or scarf.
CHIPPY:	a carpenter.
COMPOSITE CAR:	a car with mixed class accommodation.
COUPE:	a closed compartment in the cars.
CORNICE:	an ornamental moulding on the roof of the cars.
DOWN(SIDE):	that line of the railway running away from London.
GAUGE-RESTRICTED:	unable to pass over certain parts of the railway system as too big, long or heavy for that particular part.
IN TRAFFIC:	while actually running in service.
LIVE-RAIL:	the third rail (on Southern Lines) carrying electricity to motors in the train.

REQUISITION:	a written internal order for a part needed in the repairing/ refurbishing process.
ROAD:	a railway track.
SALOON:	the interior compartment(s) of the cars.
SIDE-LIGHTS:	the side windows of the cars.
SPUR:	a siding, but also the name of the tracks which run from Preston Park to Hove, "the Cliftonville Spur".
SQUARE ANGLE:	a T-Square.
STEP-TREADS:	raised and stippled metal edging to the steps into the cars to give better foot-grip.
STOCKS:	a wooden framework to support an object such as a car during construction.
STOCK NUMBER:	each part of a Pullman car was given a number for identification when needed for the repairing/refurbishing process (see REQUISITION).
SUPPLEMENTARY TICKETS:	tickets issued by the Company to cover additional expenses on top of the main fare.
TENDER:	a special carriage for coal and water, attached to the rear of a steam-locomotive.
TIE-BARS:	cross pieces of metal to strengthen a truck or similar structure.
TONGUE-AND-GROOVE:	board with projecting tenon to fit into a groove in a matching board.
TRUSS-BARS:	heavy cross members in a bogie truck.
UNDERFRAME:	the heavy frame of the car which supported the body and held the bogies.
UP(SIDE):	that line of the railway running to London.
VESTIBULE:	the enclosed space at the end of a car giving access to the seating areas and passage between the cars.
WOODMAN:	coach-builder or cabinet maker.

Dr Beeching

There's a former "Railway Workshop" to the north of Lover's Walk

There's redundant craftsmen in the town

And when they meet, they stop and talk

Of the day that Dr Beeching closed them down.

He was known as Dr Beeching and his plans were far outreaching

He closed down Lancing works as well

And this former City Slicker

Snatched away Lord Ollies' kipper

When he went and dumped the good old 'Brighton Belle'.

Across the 'Herring Pond' and in places far beyond

The name of Pullman meant 'perfection'

But Beeching came and waved his wand

And scattered them in each direction.

He said, "To make the railways viable, we must be more reliable

Think of the millions that we can save"

But when Dr Beeching finished, the 'Railways' were diminished

George Mortimer Pullman, turned over in his grave.

Don Carter.

ABOUT THIS BOOK

This book was made by: Al Deakin, Mike Hayler, Nick Wellings and Tom Woodin. Thanks to Ruth Sykes.

Thanks to Marilyn Clay for the cover design. Contact Marilyn Clay, 34a Upper North Street, Brighton. Tel. 204611.

Photographs by Joe Kent.

Published by QueenSpark Books, 68 Grand Parade, Brighton BN2 2JY. April 1992.

Printed by Delta Press, South Wing, Level One, New England House, New England Street, Brighton, BN1 4GH.

ISBN No: 0 904733 50 5.

ABOUT QUEENSPARK

QueenSpark is a community writing and publishing group based in Brighton. We believe that anyone who wants to can be a writer and our aim is to encourage and publish writing by people who do not normally get into print. QueenSpark is not a commercial company. We have some part-time paid workers, but most of us are volunteers who work together to write and produce books, gaining and sharing skills and confidence as we go.

We have a number of active writing workshops in Brighton and Hove, women only and mixed groups. Our manuscripts group reads all manuscripts, decides which ones to publish, and sets up a book making group for each publication. All groups are run on a cooperative basis and are free. Membership of QueenSpark is £5 waged or £3 unwaged per annum. If you would like to get involved, ring Brighton 571916, or write to QueenSpark Books, 68 Grand Parade, Brighton BN2 2JY.

QueenSpark is a member of the national Federation of Worker Writers and Community Publishers. If you live outside Brighton we can give you the address of your nearest Federation group and information on the books they publish. QueenSpark gratefully acknowledges funding from South East Arts, Brighton Borough Council and Hove Borough Council.

QUEENSPARK BOOK LIST

Since the early 1970's we have been publishing books, mainly local autobiographies, but also books of humour, poetry, history and politics. Many of them have sold out one or more editions. The following are currently in print:

1. *Poverty, Hardship but Happiness - Those were the days, 1903-1917.* Albert Paul (1974, 1975, 1981). The story of a Brighton working class boy's life early this century. Price £1.50.

3. *TheTown Beehive - A young girl's lot in Brighton 1910-1934.* Daisy Noakes (1975,1980,1992). The story of her childhood and years in service. A special insight into the life of women in Brighton earlier this century. Price £3.00.

7. *Live and Learn: a life and struggle for progress.* Les Moss (1979). One man's trade union and political activism in London and Brighton from the 1920's onward. Price £1.50.

9. *Hard Times and Easy Terms.* Bert Healey (1980). The entertaining life story of a Queens Park cockney and wide boy. Price £1.50

10. *The Landlord Commeth.* Jack Cummings (1981). The story of a London labour activist and conscientious objector who goes off to the First World War. Price £1.50.

12. *Hard Work and No Consideration: 51 years as a carpenter-joiner 1917-1968.* Albert Paul (1981). Vividly describes his working life in Brighton, and around England during the War. Price £1.50.

13. *Who Was Harry Cowley?* QueenSpark (1984). The controversial biography of a Brighton chimney sweep and local legend, known as The 'Gov'nor'. Price £1.50.

14. *Who Stood Idly By...* Alf Johns (1984). A book of humourous and political poems and cartoons by a retired hospital porter. Price £1.50.

16. *Growing up in Ditchling.* Doris Hall (1985, 1991). abeautifully illustrated account of girlhood in a Sussex rural village during the wars. Price £3.95.

19. *One Camp in the Living Room: a woman's life in Rottingdean.* Margaret Ward (1988). A women's life behind the facade of a Sussex seaside village. Price £1.95

20. *Backyard Brighton.* QueenSpark Books and the Lewis Cohen Urban Studies Centre at Brighton Polytechnic (1988, 1991). A book of photo's and memories of Brighton houses which were demolished in the 1930's. Price £4.95.

21. *Everything seems Smaller: a Brighton Boyhood Between the Wars.* Sid Manville (1989). A vivid account of growing up in Bear Road, Brighton between the wars. Price £2.50.

22. *Backstreet Brighton.* QueenSpark Books and the Lewis Cohen Urban Studies Centre at Brighton Polytechnic (1989). Photographs taken by Brighton Borough Council as a record of houses scheduled for demolition (1950's and 60's), with reminiscences of people who lived in them. Price £3.95.

23. *Moulsecoomb Days - Learning and Teaching on a Brighton Council Estate 1922-1947.* Ruby Dunn (1990). Traces the embattled creation of community in a 'garden suburb' without so much as a school or church. Price £2.50.

24. *Brighton Behind the Front.* QueenSpark Books and the Lewis Cohen Urban Studies Centre at Brighton Polytechnic (1990). Photographs and reminiscences of life in Brighton during the Second World War. Price £3.95.

25. *Writers Reign.* QueenSpark writing groups. (1991). A lively anthology of poetry and prose. Price £3.90.

26. *Blighty Brighton.* QueenSpark Books and the Lewis Cohen Urban Studies Centre at Brighton Polytechnic (1991). Photographs and reminiscences of life in Brighton during the First World War. Price £4.95.

27. *Pullman Craftsmen.* Don Carter, Joe Kent , Geoff Hart. Ed. by Nick Wellings (1992). An entertaining history of life in the Brighton Pullman works as seen through the eyes of three old hands.

28. *Daring Hearts.* Brighton Ourstory Group. (1992) A lesbian and gay oral history of Brighton in the 50's and 60's. Price £5.95.

Reminiscence pack. A pack of photographs and slides of Brighton this century. May be borrowed free of charge by OAP and community group. The slides cover themes such as childhood, leisure, housing, transport and WW2. Pack of 110 slides costs £50.

Education packs. Two illustrated education packs based on the books by Albert Paul and Doris Hall. Fun approaches to introduce pupils from eight upwards to the ways children's lives have changed this century. Price £3.00

QueenSpark Market Books: a number of short and cheap (all priced £1 at present) books are now on sale. These include:

Pullman Attendant, Bert Hollick: a vivid description of a waiter's life on the Pullman cars in the 1930's.

At the Pawnbrokers, Lillie Morgan: a vivid and amusing portrayal of working in a Brighton pawnbrokers during the First World War.

Little Ethel's Story, told by herself: a true romance set in Sussex and Brighton.

HOW TO BUY QUEENSPARK BOOKS

You can order our books by post. Write to us at QueenSpark Books, 68 Grand Parade, Brighton BN2 2JY or phone Brighton 571916 for an order form. Add 60p for each book to cover postage and packing and make cheques payable to QueenSpark Books. On weekdays our books can be bought from the Lewis Cohen Urban Studies Centre at Brighton Polytechnic on the ground floor of 68 Grand Parade, Brighton. They are on sale at local bookshops and our stall in Brighton's Upper Gardener Street Market on Saturdays. A free publications list is available on request.

INAUGURATION OF THE "QUEEN OF SCOTS"
MONDAY, 5th JULY, 1948

Menu

Le Cocktail des Epicures
ou
Le Potage Carême

Le Saumon du Tay Glacèe en Belle Vue
ou
Le Poulet de Grain Rôti à l'Ecossaise
Les Pommes Nouvelles   Les Petit Pois à la Menthe
Salade Vert

Le Parfait Bon Voyage
ou
Le Fromage du Pays   Toast Melba

Le Café

Luncheon 4/-   *Coffee 6d*

Opposite: Lunch time sweet stall at Preston Park Works with Ernie Sweetman (!) serving. On the right, Ted Browning, while on the left one of the apprentices, Derek Tanner.

Back cover: in front of a 'Brighton Belle' car in 1963. Back L. to R.: Percy Brockman, Bob West, Alf Gee, Les Nichols, Alf Clayton, Cyril Pearson. Middle L. to R.: Dennis Yeates, Ben Farr, Ted Phillips, Bert Baldwin. Front L. to R.: Alf Reeves, Ernie Smith, Tom Vinall, Fred Crayton.